Marked States

Volume 1

Toward Repurposing Mind
The Metaspheric Perspective

James Guy

Volume 1
Toward Repurposing Mind. The Metaspheric Perspective
James Guy

Marked States Series Editor
Randolph Dible

randolphdible@gmail.com
https://randolphdible.com

Toward Repurposing Mind
The Metaspheric Perspective

James Guy

© Individual author and College Publications 2024. All rights reserved.

ISBN 978-1-84890-458-3

Disclaimer: At this writing LSD is a Schedule-I substance; unlicensed possession and ingestion is against federal law. Tim Leary said: *"Don't take LSD ...unless you are specifically prepared to go out of your mind."* Alan Watts added the advice to those who did go out of their mind: *"If you get the message, hang-up the phone... go away and work on what you have seen."* The information in this book is for educational, historical, and cultural interest only and should not be construed as advocacy for or against ingestion of LSD or other psychedelics. Neither the author nor the publisher assumes any responsibility for physical, psychological, or social consequences resulting from the ingestion of these substances or their derivatives.

College Publications
Scientific Director: Dov Gabbay
Managing Director: Jane Spurr

http://www.collegepublications.co.uk

Cover design by Laraine Welch

All rights reserved. No part of this publication may be reproduced, stored in a retrieval system or transmitted in any form, or by any means, electronic, mechanical, photocopying, recording or otherwise without prior permission, in writing, from the publisher.

DEDICATION

To
MY WIFE MARY
PARTNER AND BELOVED
WHO HAS COMPANIONED ME IN THESE YEARS
OF SPIRITUAL COMMUNION

And who found this quote
which expressed her understanding of this book:

"What an extraordinary change takes place...
when for the first time the fact that everything depends
upon how a thing is thought first enters the consciousness,
when, in consequence, thought in its absoluteness
replaces an apparent reality."

– Søren Kierkegaard, 1830 Journal

Preface

It is not necessary to go out of your mind to reflexively see how mind works. But for many in the psychedelic '60's who, like me, did go out of their mind, *"...your perspective on yourself and your life is radically changed."* For me it took decades to integrate this shattering change. An entirely new model of mind was necessary. A quote from Alan Watts' book *The Joyous Cosmology*, about his own entheogenic session, may give you a sense of my motive: *"If you get the message, hang up the phone, go away and work on what you have seen."* Of those accidental mystics since then, some have published what they have seen, but very few have included the "work," as I have done here—going beyond personal integration into a breadth of research leading to a virtual collaboration with the outlier genius of thinkers in phenomenology such as G. Spencer-Brown and the intuitive simplicity of his *"unmarked"* and **"marked states."**

A peculiar thing about this book, any book, is that it is a mechanism uncomfortably similar to the organism reading it: Notice that your spine is aligned with the spine of the book and that you are bound in the same way the book is bound. You cannot stand anywhere other than between the verso and recto pages of the book, similarly between the left hand and right hand side of the body. You can turn the page, but your position does not change relative to the open book. And no matter how you try to sneak around a page to read the back of it, you are again positioned or bound in the same paradigm, over and over, regardless of how many pages you leaf at a time or in a single turn.

You cannot escape being caught in this simple circumstance, this uncomfortable confinement. With just these two comparisons: binding spine, and confining paradigm, any book begins to *feel* a lot like *mind,* with seemingly no way out of the predicament. Yet, the mystic sees a way out, and it is amazingly simple. In closing the book you are liberated (unbound)—no longer confined in that way, but now observing mind, the book, from some transcendent territory. Test this discovery; test the work, test mind, from your new and liberated position.

There is also a peculiar thing about the way in which you likely first browsed this book—impatiently, perhaps a quick read of the back cover, or simply thumbing the pages and images. What you may not realize is that those choices come out of an evolutionary prime directive in mind: to get beyond the uncomfortable moments of not knowing what something is about.

In everyday life this directive compels mind to identify not knowing as a nagging discomfort, something to be resolved quickly, for mind apparently abhors unknowing—needing to figure life out entertainingly like a whodunit novel or movie, or heuristically like this book, or urgently like civilization depends on it. That impulse to do it quickly and instinctively originated as the saber-toothed cat or "other" confronted early man on a hunting trail and the decision whether to fight or flee had to be made. It is this nagging discomfort and that confining paradigm of mind itself, along with a mix of fear, ecstasy, confusion, and finally understanding, which compelled me to pursue this work.

Contents

Preface **Peculiar thing about this book...** vii

PartOne **Losing Mind** THE BACKSTORY:
AN ACCIDENTAL MYSTIC AND THE METASPHERIC PERSPECTIVE **1-43**

THE set and setting .... WHAT THE SENATE HEARING DID NOT HEAR   2-3

THE politics OF ecstasy .... AND THE WAR ON CONSCIOUSNESS   4-5

THE back door of mind...................... AND ITS 500 MICROGRAM KEY   6-7

THE entheogenic vision .... AND I WAS IT   8-9

THE front door OF mind ....HAD DEFINITELY BEEN LEFT AJAR   10-11

THE initiation.. AND THE MAYONNAISE JAR   12-13

THE invitation .... TIM'S KIND LETTER   14-15

THE dance ....SHOULD I GO WITH IT? TIM SAYS YES   16-17

THE flashback.. AND THE HIGHWAY TO OBLIVION   18-19

THE surrender event .... AND THE GRACE OF PRESENCE   20-21

THE felt message .... GODHOOD AND EGOHOOD   22-23

THE mistake OF identity..THE COSMIC JOKE   24-25

THE dilemma resolved.................................. AND CHOGYAM TRUNGPA RINPOCHE   26-27

THE septenary art of tantra .... AND THE KUNDALINI CHAKRAS   28-29

THE esoteric anatomy.........................THE YOGA ONE DOES IS NOT THE YOGA   30-31

THE neurology of bliss .... NOT LIMITED TO ORGASM   31-33

THE quantum biology..THE DOWNSIDE AND UPSIDE   34-35

THE informed psyche .... THE HEART MATRIX   36-37

THE whole picture .... IT IS NOT ONLY ABOUT THE BRAIN   38-39

THE new culture .... REMEMBER: BE HERE NOW   40-41

THE metaculture .... TOWARD REPURPOSING SELF-FIRST MIND   42-43

PartTwo **Acquiring Mind** THE GREY PAPER:
PHENOMENOLOGY AND THE METASPHERIC PERSPECTIVE **45-79**

THE acquisition OF language .... MALCOLM DAVID LOWE   46-47

THE acquisition OF number .... 1ST 2ND 3RD PERSON DEIXIS   48-49

THE verbal curtain OF mind .... TIMOTHY LEARY   50-51

THE undifferentiated one .... AND SCRIPTURA CONTINUA   52-53

THE acquisition OF sign .... CHARLES S. PEIRCE   54-55

THE hidden sign .... AT THE HEART OF METASPHERE   56-57

THE conative mode OF mind .... OR "AUTOMATIC THOUGHT"   58-59

THE booting up .... THAT UNGROUNDED FEELING   60-61

THE first distinction .... G. SPENCER-BROWN AND RANDY DIBLE   62-63

THE virtual headgear .... EYE TO "I" ANALOGUE   64-65

THE **metasphere** .... THE SYNERGY OF DISTINCTIONS, SIGN, AND THE ARC   66-67

THE reflexive universe .... ARTHUR M. YOUNG   68-69

THE arc of process .... AND ITS APPLICATION BY YOUNG   70-71

THE seven categories OF ideas .... PETER MARK ROGET   72-73

THE nullstate .... AND SEPTENARY SYMMETRY IN MYTH   74-75

THE nullpoint .... AS AN ESCAPEMENT MECHANISM   76-77

THE point .... THE NULLPOINT AND VIEWPOINT   78-79

PartThree **Repurposing Mind** THE GAME MANUAL
THE APPLICATION OF METASPHERIC PERSPECTIVE **81-93**

THE gameboard 82-83

THE unmarked space, THE first distinction(s), THE apparent "I" 84-85

THE turning point, apprehension of appearance, ordinary play 86-87

THE discontinuous "I," THE unmarked "gap" 88-89

THE initial thoughts, THE afterthoughts 90-91

THE script of the game, THE summary formula, THE endgame 92-93

Tribute To the League of Students & Masters of the Game
IN PARTICULAR HERMANN HESSE AND TIMOTHY LEARY, AND THE OTHERS **95-111**

Hermann Hesse and Timothy Leary......... THE POET OF THE INNER JOURNEY 95-102

C. Michael Smith Ph.D. .... SCHOLARLY REVIEW   103

Jakob Böhme..THE "PHILOFOFIC GLOBE"   104

Buckminster Fuller... "MINIMUM UNIVERSE"   105

René Daumal.. THE SURREAL UNIVERSE   105

Melvil Dewey.................. THE "CLASSIFICATORY" POLLUTION OF METADATA   106

Peter Mark Roget .... THE "CATEGORICAL" IMPERATIVE   107

Franklin Jones .... THE KNEE OF LISTENING   108

Adi Da Samraj... THE "ILLUSION OF DIFFERENCE"   109

Felice Varini .... THE ANAMORPHIC EYE IN ART & NATURE   110

Charles S. Peirce .... "QUASI MIND" AND THE PHENOMENOLOGY OF LIGHT   111

Reference
Selected Bibliography 115-119

Index to Illustrations and Panels   121

Previous Publications, Recent Presentation Venues, Author Contact..   123

§

Part One
Losing Mind

THE BACKSTORY:

AN ACCIDENTAL MYSTIC AND THE METASPHERIC PERSPECTIVE

There was nothing haphazard or accidental about the day in 1965 this author purposely took a potent 500μg dose of LSD. After all, I had prepared for the trip for a couple of years, even the whole course of my life of 25 years. Now, many decades later, that experiential *loss of mind* will serve the reader as a backstory to how mind is acquired, its evolutionary purpose, and how that purpose has everything to do with personal and global crises.

The trip turned out to be one of those reality-shattering events commonly told among my contemporaries in the "psychedelic 60's." Yet when told today, in the "psychedelic renaissance," such reality-shattering events are barely heard above the murmuring of neuropsychologists touting micro doses of "Schedule-I" psychedelics for a range of modern disorders, from chain smoking to PTSD.

For students of the new and old schools of consciousness, here is a first-hand account of what traditionally has been called the reality-shattering mystic event, which today might be called the unitive or non-dual experience.

The session itself lasted 12 hours, yet its effect on body and mind lasted for years—a mix of ecstasy, fear, confusion and finally, a decade later—understanding. A year into all this, I surprisingly found myself friends with Tim Leary.

At Tim's kind invitation, I joined him at Millbrook in 1966, for what turned out to be another shattering event, which, on return home, triggered years of intense episodes of Kundalini-Shakti. You should know that I now neither advocate nor oppose entheogen use, rather align with Alan Watts' book on his psychedelic experience, *The Joyous Cosmology:*

"If you get the message, hang up the phone. For psychedelic drugs are simply instruments, like microscopes, telescopes, and telephones. The biologist does not sit with an eye permanently glued to the microscope. He goes away and works on what he has seen."

And certainly, neither "the message" nor "the work" are the same for everyone. Yet, we can infer in Watts' tone that the message is extremely important new information previously unimaginable, perhaps intimately revealing, beautifully ecstatic, or even terrifying. In any case, there remains the admonition: **"He goes away and works on what he has seen."**

Toward Repurposing (self-first) *Mind* is my *"work"* on what I have seen, not only in the twelve hours of the LSD session, but over the many decades since. It is a discovery of someone who had the nagging discomfort of wanting to know something more about mind and consciousness, self and other, than what ordinarily comes to mind.

Spoiler alert: This is not a primer on air pollution, the climate, fall of civilizations, nor on psychedelics. It is a treatise on *mind*—a new way to understand that it is the **way**, or *how*, we think, not **what** we think that causes both personal and global crises, notably the climate crisis. It first examines the *affectual life* after a reality-shattering realization like *losing mind,* and by extension, how mind was first acquired. It is as wide-ranging a conversation as these few pages can accommodate and perhaps as controversial as any literary attempt to integrate the extremes of duality and non-duality just long enough to bridge the chasms of philosophical, scientific, cultural, and personal bias— to discover the source of *bias* itself, or mind it*self,* in these three easy parts:

PartOne, the backstory: LSD and my participation in the 60's psychedelic culture, including integration of the feeling energy of consciousness, or bliss.

PartTwo, a paper on a phenomenological model of how mind is *acquired,* its *purpose* and the *flaw* in that purpose.

PartThree, a practice manual and game model purposed toward repurposing the evolutionary self-first *flaw* in mind.

This first part is told in the order in which the events and experiences unfolded. Along the way are historical or technical references giving definition and context to the unfolding.

As for how I decided on that 500 micrograms of LSD: that was the recommended dose for a breakthrough event according to the psychedelic research going on in 1960-1962 at Harvard with Dr. Timothy Leary and Dr. Richard Alpert, at the helm of what was called the "*Psilocybin Project"* and another called the "*Good Friday Experiment."*

Tim started these projects shortly after he had returned from a trip to Cuernavaca, Mexico, where, at the recommendation of a friend, he consumed ceremonial mushrooms (psilocybin in the raw). Tim would later recount in a 1965 filmed interview:

"I learned more about psychology in the five hours after taking these mushrooms than in the preceding 15 years of studying and doing [academic and clinical] research in psychology."

As most readers know, Leary's academic track took a sharp turn, as the *Psilocybin Project* ran aground and Tim was fired from Harvard in 1963 for *"...absenting himself from Cambridge without permission."* Shortly before that, Alpert had been fired for *"having given an undergraduate a psychedelic off campus."* With Harvard no longer having their back, they went underground. Ralph Metzner joined Tim and Richard at Millbrook (a 2000 acre estate in up state New York). Metzner continued as editor of the *Psychedelic Review.* And as an early subscriber to that journal, and before taking LSD myself, I was probably more informed than the general public about what Leary was up to.

As the academic curtain came down on psychedelic research, so too the politics of consciousness gave way to criminalizing psychedelic science. All such research and experimentation went underground for the next fifty years (including the goings-on at Millbrook), which coincide with the unfolding of the phenomenological non-drug discoveries in this book. But resolving the politics and science of psychedelics is not within the scope of this book.

Before going too far underground, it was Timothy Leary who had the first and last opportunity, on behalf of us all, to explain psychedelics to a Senate Hearing Committee in 1966:

"The challenge of the psychedelic chemicals is not just how to control them, but how to use them." -T.L.

After hours of testimony, Tim implored congress not to criminalize psychedelic use, which he knew would put in place a reverse psychology, which would have the effect of removing the safeguards proper *"set and setting"* and harm reduction protocol that his research showed otherwise provide.

My own concern loudly echoes Leary's prediction, especially in light of the current casual regard for the power of psychedelics evidenced in mostly uninformed comment strings in social media groups with psychedelic, LSD, Psilocybin, or DMT in the group's name. I too implore my audience, in particular the younger members of the psychedelic culture, not to dabble. Do serious research. At least find out exactly what Tim meant by "*set and setting.*"

My own curiosity was never on the casual, or so-called *"recreational,"* side of the '60's psychedelic culture, nor do I believe, even after hundreds of max-dose sessions between them, that it was Leary and Alpert's interest. Eventually they got *"the message"* and began *"the work."* Richard left Millbrook first to meet his guru and follow the traditional mystic or yogic path. Leary remained the revolutionary, persecuted and praised, bent on finding the answer in the brain, virtual reality, and futurism. Metzner pursued shamanism.

What is "set and setting?"

*"Of course, the drug dose does not produce the transcendent experience. It merely acts as a chemical key; it opens the mind, frees the nervous system of its ordinary patterns and structures. The nature of the experience depends almost entirely on set and setting. **Set** denotes the preparation of the individual, including his personality structure and his mood at the time. **Setting** is physical, the weather, the room's atmosphere; social, feelings of persons present towards one another; and cultural, prevailing views as to what is real.*

*Social support networks have shown to be particularly important in the outcome of the psychedelic experience. They are able to control or guide the course of the experience, both consciously and subconsciously. A **setting** of stress, fear, or a disagreeable environment, may result in an unpleasant experience (bad trip). Conversely, a relaxed, curious person in a warm, comfortable and safe place is more likely to have a pleasant experience."*

Alpert in a video interview after being fired from the Harvard Corporation

Dr. Richard Alpert, aka Ram Dass, 1931-2019

These men are gone now, but not before I had the privilege of their good company. Here is a recollection of my first visit to Millbrook in 1965, a month or so before my LSD session, and several months before my friendship with Tim and Ralph. At this time Richard Alpert was facilitating Castalia at Millbrook summer workshops. This was two years before he went to India and reluctantly met his guru Neem Karoli Baba and received his yogic devotee name, Ram Dass (Servant of God).

After a quiet welcome by staff at the Poughkeepsie train station and a half hour car ride to Millbrook, I found myself along with the other attendees gathered in a large room in the 60 room Victorian mansion. We were all being seated on the floor around several makeshift coffee tables across from Alpert and his motley crew, who were already seated. I searched their faces and body language for some inkling of their psychedelic realization; it seemed guarded. I listened intently to Alpert's soothing speech, entranced by his calm collected manner, perhaps typical of a Harvard man, but, with a touch of bewilderment.

My own character *(set)* was typical of a quiet responsible 25 year old advertising art director. But perhaps not so typical had been my avocational interest in the ancient teachings around the *mystic experience*, which, along with the news about the psychedelic experience, had brought me to Millbrook.

In anticipation of the day I might receive the promised illumination I had done my homework—reading the *Psychedelic Review*, and tracking the Harvard scandal. I thought myself prepared and ready to imbibe the magic elixir.

I left Millbrook a psychedelic virgin.

Photo: Castalian vision at Millbrook, circa 1966

Castalia at Millbrook
In one attempt to accommodate their exile from academic bias, Leary settled in Zihuatanejo, Mexico, for all of 6 weeks before authorities told him he was not welcome. Then, as fate might have it, Leary was offered hermitage on a 2000+ acre estate that his new millionaire friend Billy Hitchcock offered for $500/mo. Located near the Village of Millbrook in upstate New York, just east of Poughkeepsie, this was ideal seclusion and ample space for community in a 60 room mansion with other smaller buildings on the sprawling property. Leary and Alpert moved into the big vacant house along with a handful of devoted friends. And from 1963 to 1968 the property hosted hundreds of people—doctors, lawyers, hippies, and priests, in their pilgrimage from all over the world, seeking instruction and guidance in the art of consciousness. I have since seen images of the Millbrook Big House, with the sacred graffiti you see in this photo painted over, as if to white wash the discoveries that came to mind 50 years ago.

For those closest to the question, there were conflicting voices out there, as to whether it was wise to even consider taking LSD. Likewise, the question how do I get my hands on some? Although nothing I was hearing was deterring me from my quest, I did have to step out of my comfort zone, my *"quiet responsible lifestyle,"* and get down on the streets, where there was already a savvy psychedelic culture, one that could fix you up. Long story short, I wangled a stash of a dozen clean and measured 250µg dose capsules of LSD from the neighborhood chemist, in spite of his long drawn out paranoid and teasing behavior, even though LSD was only rumored illegal. It was as late as 1966 when it became illegal in Nevada and California, and nationwide in 1968.

By 1966 Leary's own voice was loud, but not so clear, when he said *"Turn on, tune in, drop out"*—the *"drop out"* part is still misunderstood and so similar to Alan Watts' *"got the message... do the work."* Whether *"Tricky Dick"*[1] actually said Leary was *"the most dangerous man in America"* is questionable, but unquestionable is that it was the general political misunderstanding of what Leary was up to.

"Don't take LSD unless you are very well prepared, unless you are specifically prepared to go out of your mind. Don't take it unless you have someone that's very experienced with you to guide you through it. And don't take it unless you are ready to have your perspective on yourself and your life radically changed, because you're gonna be a different person, and you should be ready to face this possibility." –Timothy Leary, CBC documentary, 1966

FIRST NEWS OF THE RESEARCH

Under Ralph Metzner's editorial tenure and with consulting editors like Stanley Krippner, Alan Watts, and Huston Smith, and at only $2 an issue, this publication was my first connection to the new science and philosophy of psychedelics. In a 1966 issue Leary first explained his appropriation of Hermann Hesse's 25th century vision of Castalia. *[See Tribute, pp 95-102]*

FIRST MANUAL FOR THE CULTURE

1964

A manual based on the Tibetan Book of The Dead by Timothy Leary, Richard Alpert, and Ralph Metzner.

The book was published less than a year before I took LSD. Although I was reading everything I could get my hands on, such as the Journal above, I decided not to read this book, for it was in said journal that I read a review of the book and decided I did not want the book to possibly reset my "set" with talk of the "bardos" in death and rebirth. I did read the book several years after my session.

Here is a link to Gerald Heard's review of The Psychedelic Experience *Re-Birth Without Fear*

http://maps.org research-archive/psychedelicreview/v1n5/015110lea.pdf

---

[1] President Richard Nixon.

One evening, months after I had returned from the Millbrook workshop, I heard an abrupt knock on my boarding house room door. The landlady told me: *"There are two gentlemen downstairs."* I invited them up. They had heard about Millbrook and got my address from Lisa B's Castalia Foundation at Millbrook mailing list. It seems I was the only listing for Cincinnati. Anyway, we were excited to meet each other. They told me their only experience with psychedelics was getting sick on morning glory seeds. I confessed I was a psychedelic virgin, but I did have some LSD. They responded *"What are you waiting for?"* My patience had finally been rewarded. I had found people who Leary might call "guides," or what are now called *"sitters."*

Although these were strangers, I went with my intuition to trust them and trust my *"set"* of 25 years of preparedness. We decided on early morning on a weekend at their home as the *"setting."* I followed Leary's research and took two tiny white capsules from my newly acquired stash.

I was about to turn the key to the back door of mind, drastically altering the spiritual and bodily course of my life, just as Leary had warned us all.

Everyone *sitting* in on a session influences its course and, hopefully, the benefit of the session. I was the only one ingesting the LSD. I sat back quietly to watch what came to mind. The room was quiet, with no music or extraordinary decor. Soon my attention was sent to body sensations and becoming more and more aware of a background tension that ordinarily might be unnoticed, yet eventually became amplified to the point of considerable discomfort.

I had started out sitting on a comfortable sofa, but feeling increased tension, I slithered to the floor to get my back as flat as possible. I began to see the effects manifest. Ordinary imperfections and cracks in the walls became beautiful matrices of neon colored lines. Each pattern stacking and shifting organically, as if I were seeing the real appearance of things as more open or empty space than substance. The furniture seethed, the carpet rippled, the walls became transparent, revealing a dark and spacious matrix of brilliant color, spaces and shapes.

A dance of particles of light went on in the foreground. Physical or bodily connection to all of these *other* objects became unquestionably apparent. The ambiance was all somehow familiar.

It seems important to give the reader as detailed a description as I can recall, so that there builds a notion of context in which discovery at any level or under any condition of mind can be compared to, so-called, normal consciousness. There is no dreaming going on here. Likewise, no hard or even soft *reasoning* going on either.

I felt protected enough in the *setting,* to eventually close my eyes. I believe I spent most of the trip that way. Here, too, there builds a notion that there is no interior that is not exterior, no outside that is not inside. Of course, my comments here are in retrospect. I was not doing any such, even tacit, analyzing in the midst of the experience itself. Which is not to dismiss flashes of tacit, non-verbal realization that came to mind. When eyes were open, I saw three different people in the room, each at different times. These were my newly acquainted *guides.*

Though none of us were experienced, lucky for me, in my now fragile psychedelic condition, these strangers handled the whole session with ethical and compassionate care. I recall a remarkable flash of insight that occurred at some point about these people silently walking around the room. It was an immediate and profound realization about *"the other"* or others in general:

*They (**these others**) were merely an apprehension of my own person-ality and could, should, and would vanish as mere thought. These were not entities.*

There was also a woman, whom I had not met previous to her sudden presence in an easy chair, looking down at me as I lay sprawled on the floor. Her form appeared distorted, plastic, impersonal, but, as I had been doing with other surreal imagery, I intuitively ignored her disfigurement: a bloated belly, a frown of agonizing concern, even her fragrance, as just part of the magic theatre that I was now in. No one spoke to me, and it seemed all of them carefully avoided speaking *about me*, at least not where I could hear them.

My intuition was to not give much importance to particular hallucinations about my surroundings. Of course in the midst of it these were not hallucinations; this was reality. They were what these supposedly material objects "really" look like: transparent, shifting fields of energy and light, a dynamic matrix of reality. However, my chronic attention was on the extreme tension in my neck and back. I thought to myself: what if this knot, this contraction, grows so painful as to become unbearable?

Then, at the most painful tension, everything exploded into colorful particles of pleasurable *bliss*. I was carried along in an overwhelming ecstatic sensual flow, penetrating the skin, bones, and mind, including the furniture. Utter, total relaxation extended into the bliss. Meanwhile, objects had added to their repertoire a brilliant warm light. I found myself forcefully, joyfully in love-bliss with everything in the room.

Without rational thought at the time, I can say now I "felt" what that word "bliss" truly means. These new feelings, sensations and realizations were inexplicably very familiar, somehow.

Experimenting, I began interacting with and getting pleasurably physically *entangled* in the furniture, falling through carpet and floor. I felt these objects as *field*, not solid, and as continuation of my own body and limb. I was falling head over heels through the pleasurable flux of existence. Everything was in flow. Existence had always been in flow, never not flowing. Even when I was not moving, the ecstatic flow continued around me, through me, and beyond the room into a feeling of a vast unseen panorama of cosmic space. I recall saying out loud:

"SO THIS IS IT!"

...as if others in the room were experiencing that same thing, and would answer. It also occurred to me that it was all a "game," a **Godhood** play.

I laughed out loud, almost hysterically, at the "cosmic joke"—what an introduction to reality!

On the serious side, it occurred to me that humankind (those present in the room), the universe, all had been waiting for me to arrive *here*, so that they could get on with "it"— with what, I was never sure. Such intuitions of liability and responsibility probably continued for a time. However, such intuition faded after a time. My feeling, even now, is difficult to describe in relation to time. The whole trip could have happened in a period of minutes, hours, centuries even millennia.

At some point after many of these *Godhood* adventures, most of which I cannot recall, the room became the entire cosmos—all realms, illusory and otherwise, and **I WAS IT!**

Just prior to that glorious illumination, the room had quieted even more; my body, the cosmos—all was deathly, blissfully quiet. My whole awareness was the bliss and background buzzing and hissing of lucid blackness, apparently all contained, including myself, in a curved tetrahedral shape of the cosmos. Floating there in perfect bliss, I then began to rise and accelerate through an iris-like opening in the surface of the shape of space. It occurred to me that:

Existence is this infinite expanding surface upon an infinite expanding void entering into a greater infinite void.

Luminous stuff was falling behind in my wake as I entered the blackness of the opening–ever outward. The universe was expansion of what was into what is.

I had arrived at a brilliantly lighted, perfectly shaped room.

Everything curved in on itself. The room was the all and all of a bliss-filled universe. There were doors and windows, but I intuited that even if I opened them, the way out would lead back into the room itself. All, including what I suppose was my body, was a seething flux of ecstatic pleasurable flow.

Eventually two immense figures enter this cosmos-size room (likely near the end of the session). They squeeze into the space—we exchange inquisitive glances. Then I reason: *"So, this must be **eternity**," simply being in this perfect room, in perfect bliss with these [others]"* ... suddenly the *fearful* thought:

NO! I DON'T WANT (pause)

Their faces suddenly turn forlorn and crush toward me.

"What have I done... thinking that thought?" **Eternity suddenly becomes a hot claustrophobic embryonic sack,** with us all inside shrinking or dropping at light speed through a bottomless tunnel of painful space.

"I am caught with this hot wet flesh of bodies for eternity."

The more struggle, the more cutting pain, like a thousand **razor cuts slicing my brain tissue**. The pain seemingly or actually lasts for *10,000 years*. Suddenly I open my eyes and someone is wiping my forehead with a wet cloth. I gratefully realize that I am sitting in what appears to be a normal kitchen.

IT'S OVER.

---

[1] As the thought began to form I blocked it. Only years later did I realize it was the ultimate egoic act of the "I" or separate self, and the opposite to love.

"Metasphere" Photo-art by author's wife, Mary.

A tetra-shaped opal in 2 inch diameter globe by Dr. Green Glassworks, Las Cruces, NM.

These photos of a found piece of art express my vision of "a perfectly shaped room in perfect bliss."

My *hosts*, my *sitters,* got me to my car. Somehow I drove home to my boarding house. I slept the remains of the weekend, got up on Monday and went to work at the ad agency.

Not unusual, given the gravity of one's experience, the psychedelia phrase **"coming down"** is used. You might come down with a thud of both realization and confusion.

In my case: down from the ineffable Godhood height of eternal love-bliss and realization that there is only one being—and confused, there at the end. As if I had failed some test of that Godhood realization of oneness or connectedness with **"the other(s)**." Had I failed in some ultimate sacrifice, some ultimate love?

In the days and months immediately following the LSD session, the **front door of mind** had definitely been left ajar. The opening allowed panic and paranoia (egohood) to have its way with me. I recall a typical auditory hallucination when I was in a crowd and someone in back of me said: *"He has no idea how much he is screwing up; we're all going down with him you know."* At the time, I was at a loss to explain such episodes of paranoia, which further increased the fear in my "dilemma." No narrative can convey the emotionally disturbing realization that at any moment I could or would dissolve into the aloneness of *"all-one-ness."* It was many years before the "dilemma" would be put to rest.

Meanwhile, here I am, months after the session, still treading the deepening waters of my dilemma, repeatedly rhetorically asking my "self":

"What am "I" supposed to do?"

All those months I was on my own, with no one I dared confide in. I found, to my severe agony and panic, that it is the trying to f*igure it all* out that is the unbearable suffering. For a year I felt without a ground, desperately trying to understand *("integrate")* the experience. There was no step within the dilemma that I could think to take that would be the right choice. But in some Atlasian paranoia, it seemed all up to me to make the right choice for humankind. A choice between the great **expansion** (like the expansion at the height of the session) or its polar opposite, the great **contraction** (like the claustrophobic descent at the end of the session).

When flashes of the dilemma demanded the choice be made, mind bent sharply and painfully away from making a choice either way, or *POOF*... my world, all worlds, the cosmos, reality itself, would surely be lost in some...

annihilating contraction, or in some unendurable expansion.

In each arising of this existential dilemma, I barely managed not to make a choice. After a year in fear of such terminal moments, I concluded *even death might not be the single end one might hope for. Nor birth that apparent single beginning one might presume*.

And after a decade *I would conclude that the "I" is merely a thought, and that "I" being fearful is its very evolutionary purpose. Thus how could (the) "I" possibly know what to do?* And later all this fearful suffering would prove to have been an unnecessary enterprise conceived in ignorance of the evolutionary purpose of the "I-self."

I came to suppose the easiest way to justify the panic that arose out of this ("bad trip"), while awaiting resolution of this interminable dilemma (integration), is to acknowledge that it is both mystically and phenomenologically *by way of the **back door** of mind that we are consumed in the bliss of Godhood, and by way of the **front door** or lion at the gate, that we are consumed in the fear and confusion of egohood.*

Whereas Godhood is otherwise considered the ultimate existential state of being, it is also, at least as far as I have experienced first-hand or first-personally, a phenomenological event.

So, "Is there only one being?"

A few weeks after the LSD session, my landlady gave me notice that the boarding house had been sold.

I fortunately found a tiny 3-room house that in its vintage time must have been a servants' quarters for a large estate, long since diffused into a middle class neighborhood.

My entrance was a long flight of steps up a hill from a seldom-traveled street. I felt this precarious dwelling was perfectly suited to my desire for hermitage or place to figure things out —a cliff side monastery, of sorts, a place to let the dilemma work itself out.

Curiously, from my front window, I could look down across the street at a nunnery. Given my state of mind, obviously I was in the right neighborhood.

After getting some furniture and settling in, I decided it best to keep my mind occupied with more than coming home from work everyday, as if nothing was going on, only to ponder this consuming dilemma.

What is Paranoia?

Another psychedelia colloquialism is the word "paranoia," not to be confused with the clinical term indicating a chronic psychological disorder. I would use the term to explain the natural facility of mind to try to *"figure it all out,"* even if that means postulating unlikely scenarios that anyone in their right mind would dismiss as the explanation of what's happening.

Likewise, in the state purposely induced by LSD there may also arise other phenomena similar to those described by clinicians in the diagnosis "psychosis" but they differ here in regard to degree and duration.

Because there is that spectrum involved here, I am hoping there can be an understanding of these phenomena with less stigma than that associated with the plethora of "clinical" terms.

Mind simply wants to figure out what the "other" or "others" are up to in direct relation to the "self" and uses the stimuli and apparent data at hand to create the most likely story.

Recall the Preface "...for mind apparently abhors unknowing—needing to..." figure things out, however absurd that figuring may appear to self".

While fearfully pondering whether I was the only being, artist that I am, I found myself chalk painting mandalas on velour paper and discarding[1] them as quickly as they were finished. After that I turned my art and inventive skill into another therapy/hobby: building a multi-media psychedelic light projector with the intention to take the contraption to Castalia someday, for their use and amusement. The project replaced my *dilemma,* which was a good thing; considering my shifted reality—it was something healthier and healing to occupy my mind.

I then had an even brighter idea: I would write to Castalia at Millbrook and invite Tim and Ralph to include Cincinnati on their upcoming '65 LSD *Lecture and Experiential Workshop tour.* To my excitement and amazement, they accepted the offer without much question. I had a couple of months to arrange a Friday night venue for Tim's public lecture at the local Unity Church. Tim asked me to do an ad, which I ran in the *Cincinnati Enquirer and Cincinnati Post* newspapers. Saturday at my tiny cliff side hermitage, Tim would hold a non-drug workshop simulating what a LSD session looks like.

LSD
LECTURE & WORKSHOP
BY
TIMOTHY: LEARY
Date, Time, and Place

Tim and Ralph graciously showed up. I picked them up at the airport and took us to my tiny home/monastery. They loved it. Tim took the upstairs bedroom. Ralph took the living room couch and I slept on the floor.

Of course, I had a hidden agenda in all this. My participation in the tour was to have the opportunity to ask Tim the question on my mind:

Are we really only one being?

Surely an answer from Tim would solve my dilemma—my suffering the past year. I felt sure he had the answer. Should I risk finding out the answer? In any case, I never found the courage to voice the question.

My small part in the Saturday workshop was to keep the appropriate sitar music playing from my reel-to-reel tape stereo system, secure the space for the duration of the event, and try not to flip out—which all proved difficult.

Behind the scenes and just before we went out from the kitchen to start the workshop, Tim pulled Ralph and me aside and produced a mayonnaise jar of clear liquid[2] from his travel bag and motioned for us each to dip our little finger down to the knuckle and lick off the residue.

All this before the government listed LSD as a Schedule-One substance. I guess this counts as my second dose of LSD. But, perhaps nowadays it would be called a *microdose,* here on micro- street in a micro middle class Cincinnati neighborhood.

The dipping into the elixir of unknown measure had come as an unexpected initiation with embarrassing results, at least for me. Eventually I felt the LSD kick in and behind a curtain where I was watching over the stereo system, Ralph's had to discretely, but actually, sit on top of me sprawled on the floor to calm a silent but very evident, to Ralph, at least, full blown flashback attack— not so much a *harm reduction* maneuver on Ralph's part, but to save us all from certain embarrassment. I somehow recovered and Ralph returned to the workshop. I continued as best I could with my assigned duties. The workshop ended with satisfied participants.

---

[1] Years later I found that Buddhists do this as a spiritual practice. [2] It may have been powder, I forget.

On Sunday, as part of the planned tour, Tim was scheduled to speak at Antioch College in Yellow Springs, Ohio, At the time, Antioch was infamous for its progressive (perhaps the word is hippie) college community, northeast of Cincinnati. Next morning I drove us all up there, a little over an hour's drive. I know that I used the time with Leary at home and on that hour or so drive, but these fifty years later I haven't a clue as to what the conversation was in the car. I do recall that we arrived several hours before Leary's scheduled talk. So we had time to meet up with the group that had organized the event. It was informal so there was some roach sharing and the pleasure of Tim's stories that everyone could not help but enjoy. My non- hippie *set* became evident as I passed on an offered toke.

Later at the event, **something happened** that typified my general state of mind, most likely an aftereffect of my informal initiation from the mayonnaise jar the previous morning. This time it was not a flashback, and I was not still high. I was standing at the back of the event auditorium, Tim was midway into his talk, and for a brief moment, I had the distinct impression I was him speaking. What was said, were my exact thoughts. Not telepathically–rather the same and shared awareness.

That leg of the tour ended and I returned my friends to the Cincinnati Airport on Monday, and afterward went on to work. Again, I was left none the wiser, not much more informed than after my visit at Millbrook with Richard Alpert. **During all that time with Tim**, I was so totally absorbed in my *egoic dilemma* and questioning of reality that to this day I cannot recall much at all of Tim's message.

> *Leary's Castalia at Millbrook:*
> In 1963, the non-profit International Federation For Internal Freedom or IFIF was disbanded and the **Castalia Foundation** was put in its stead. Leary opened the Millbrook hermitage around that time. Millbrook was the name of the place, the hermitage, but "Castalia" was its mission and vision. Leary had borrowed the name Castalia out of Hermann Hesse's Nobel Prize winning novel Das Glasperlenspiel (The Glass Bead Game), also known as Magister Ludi (Master of the Game).—A story set in the 25th century, somewhere in Europe, about a pedagogic utopian community named Castalia and the Castalian Order who were in charge of several Castalian schools around the world that played the "Glass Bead Game."
>
> Even long before the Millbrook hermitage was closed in 1968, Leary's Castalian[3] vision had vanished.

Dr. Timothy Francis Leary, 1920-1996

---

[3] More of why Leary appropriated Hesse's vision of Castalia is told in the Tribute section pp.95-111.

That same year, December, 1965, I was astonished to receive a letter from Tim thanking me for the Cincinnati hospitality and inviting me up to Millbrook for the '66 Castalia "Summer School." Excitedly, I wrote back to accept the invite, and for the intervening few months or so I worked diligently to complete the light machine as a gift to my now fellow Castalians. I thought that, rather than resign from the ad agency, I would ask for my vacation time, but remain ready to burn bridges if things worked out in New York for graphic art director career opportunities.

At last, spring came and time to head to Millbrook. I gave up my hermitage, got into my new racing green Dodge Charger, and was off to see the wizard. Everything was green, my car, the spring. Driving through the familiar Millbrook gate house was like entering the Emerald City. I was calmly excited to see the wizard again. Who knew what would be in store for the rest of my life?

They put me up in one of the newly paisley drapery decorated bedrooms—ready, I supposed, for any sessions, psychedelic or otherwise, that might arise. I was thrilled to be treated so cordially. The first night after dinner entertainment was my light machine show. They loved it. Tim called it *"The Cadillac of light machines."* I halfway regret that I no longer have that contraption, having purposely abandoned it at a 70's hippie festival in Cincinnati's Eden Park. Here at Millbrook, things were considerably changed from my earlier visit with Richard. Even the second floor exterior of the *Big House* now had Hindu religious graffiti. I don't recall if Richard was still living at Millbrook in '66. I know I did not see him while I was there.

Kundalini Tantra and Yantra symbols were painted on the massive brick chimney and a large face[1] with stoned eyes covered a good quarter of the front of the Victorian mansion.

After next day's ad hoc breakfast and more introductions all around, I took my leave and leisurely explored the house and estate. On my previous visit, most of the house had been restricted to staff. I now was staff, so I took the opportunity to check out the upper floors, showing wear and tear from long cold winters and hot summers. Out on the property, I recall, a freshly dressed deer was hanging in one of the smaller out buildings. How would I fit in? I was an *Ad Man,* not a hippie. Then I thought: Damn, Leary had been a Harvard professor and now look at him, bare foot and running a lawn mower. My mind and destiny seemed tangled amidst these people.

There were a half dozen or so leftover winter residents still holed-up in some of the various buildings, and not more than a dozen living in the Big House. Rather than bother anybody, I took a long walk in the other direction. Further up the main drive I came upon a large single floor plan house, perhaps the landlord's. No one seemed to be there so I looked into the windows. As I recall, it was spacious with stone floors dark wood carpentry, sparse decoration and an inviting rustic atmosphere. Since I had one of the few cars at Millbrook, Tim put me to work getting the daily mail and any needed groceries from town. I guess I looked like a lost puppy, and I was grateful for his attention and kindness. There was always someone wanting to go to town. I was making myself useful between lounges on the porch.

---

[1] See panel, p.4.

Box 175, Mllbrook, N.Y.

Dec 16 65

Dear B_rother Jim--

You were kind to us --and we enjoyed your house.

I am writing you now to tell you about future plans.

We leave soon for Mexico--January and February.

March 1st we return here to start getting house and grounds ready for Summer School. The school opens June 1st and runs to Aug 31.

There will be an extraordunary faculáty of talented magickans--artists, poets, philosophers etc and we plan to taansform the house into a living MUSEUM each room a session in itself.

It occured to me that you might oonsider coming. There will be some scholarship people who will be here for the spring and summer. They would be here to learn--but would get reduced rates since they would be helping out.

If you are interested in coming--anytime after March 1st through until Sept.--let me know soon. This might be a good base for you to work out connections in New Y_ork--and you would learn things that ■re not to be taught anywhere else--in these strange times.

O.K.

Have a good winter. And let us know if you are interested

Fond wishes from R_alph--

[signature]

I had been there only a few days, and one evening, long after having gone to my room, the laughter of people running through the halls awakened me. Surprisingly, they came to my room and took my hand. There were women and men, a half dozen in all, holding hands in a daisy chain. I was 26 years old, and they seemed much younger.

I uninhibitedly, but awkwardly, joined the dance, delighted to be included. I had no idea what time of night it was. **We danced like nymphs through the *Big House*.** For some reason, I said "No" when the leader of the spirited crew announced: *"Let's go to Tim's room."* I guess I thought that would be beneath Tim's stature. I am not sure if it was to answer my elderly request, but we ended up outside on the front lawn in the dark, circumambulating the big fountain. Considerable tensions came to my shoulders and at the same time a feeling of freedom. My mind was still a tangle. As I wavered between a rational state and who knows what, a girl said *"Do you think he is positive or negative?"* In a paranoid thought that I was the purpose and center of attention, I freaked as we all slumped together on the lawn in a heap of bodies and seething breath.

No one answered the girl. Silently we all lay there collapsed in exhaustion and unmoving. After a considerable time I became fearful. Was there going to be another flashback? Were they aware of the *"merging,"* the melting of bodies, that I felt? Was I holding up some cosmic orgy or event?

What was "I" supposed to do?

The answer never arrived. I suppose I blanked out.

I next found myself, of all places, in the *tower room*. I was standing there in front of Tim and Rosemary at the foot of their large floor mattress, with them on it, sitting up very still, each reading a book. I expectantly asked Tim:

"Should I go with it?"

Tim calmly asked if I had taken LSD. I answered: *"No!"*

"Yes," he said, ***"Go with it."*** I literally dove right between them on the bed. ***Thud!*** Nothing happened, nothing, and my mind immediately quieted. Then I felt more than foolish.

Tim got quickly to his feet, helped me up, and started walking me around the room. He noticed my barefoot limp and, as if to distract me, asked about it. I confessed it was hammertoe. Rosemary then said something about Tim also having hammertoe trouble.

I wish that I could recall the content of the rest of our conversation, but can only imagine that I was taken or somehow found my way back to my own room; embarrassed and exhausted.

It would seem that the question I had wanted to ask Tim, back in Cincinnati, but had not, had not only been asked but finally answered. And given the "thud" when I expected to land either in hell or in some golden clouds of Godhood, the tacit answer seems to be: *Yes, James, there is only one being, but what's the big deal? Get up and get on with it... with what, I was not quite sure.*

Next day, Tim asked me to attend to one of the retreatants left over from the winter people. She was living over the Alpine-style, 2-lane bowling alley. I was sure that she would sense my fragile state. How could that help her?

What is merging?

Most any dictionary definition of the idea or word will say: "Blend or cause to blend gradually into something else as to become indistinguishable from it, to combine or cause to combine to form a single entity."

I describe a common and most often pleasurable version of this effect in my 12-hour session, as I merged with apparently inanimate objects, dissolving into furniture, falling into the rug, the floor, and eventually into the living matrix of existence. I also describe an unpleasant version near the end of the session, where I felt entanglement with *others* and caught in a claustrophobic moment of eternal connectedness.

A more surprising event of merging (without a psychedelic) happened in the nymph dance around the Millbrook fountain, where I resisted hardily a merging with *the others*.

For some, like me, a panic, for others perhaps, an ecstatic occurrence, as in some true forms of tantric intercourse and even in common ordinary intercourse with a beloved. The difference in degree or depth is difficult to assign as we each experience reality or relationship differently.

Just what was I expected to do for her? She was petite, elderly, and handsomely beautiful, with the most graceful smile that I have ever seen on a person's face.

I had no instructions. What did I know about any of this?

She knew I was sent to comfort her in her *"coming down"* from a session, but she ended up tacitly comforting me with knowing glances. We hardly spoke and together went about ordinary housekeeping rituals in her dwelling, and then for what seems a couple of days, we simply hung out afternoons sitting in silence in the deck chairs on the Big House porch. I suppose I interrupted our sittings, running my errands for the main house, but cannot recall any particular schedule. I suppose too that most everyone who had been there through the winter months were either guests like my new deck chair friend, or regular residents. The only people I had met so far I met in the kitchen at mealtime. The whole ambiance was laid back, relaxed and quiet. I had no idea of what Millbrook was up to.

One afternoon on the porch of the mansion, my friend and I curiously watched Tim and a couple of others go into the tiny meditation building (tennis house) across the big lawn from the fountain. Neither my new companion nor I were invited, and I took comfort, even relief, in that. I imagined many scenarios of what they may have been up to in there, which even included that they might be in what today is called a *"micro dosing"* session, like we did at the Cincinnati workshop. Or maybe meditating or simply a meeting. Who knows?

Sometime later Tim and the others emerged from the tiny building and glanced over at us with knowing smiles. I suddenly imagined they were expecting something of me! A fist of energy painfully thrust at the base of my spine. I panicked. Without a word, I got up and ran. **Ran to my room** in trembling fear, grabbed my stuff, and made it to my car. I remembered the light machine, ran back and grabbed it off the front room mantel. I had so much time and labor invested in it. I found the car again and got out of there.

Days before, I had sent my boss at the ad agency a telegram, telling him I had resigned. *Oh God! Now I had burned my bridges at both ends.* I aimed the car West, toward Cincinnati, riding on a volcano of intense **fear and panic**. It was all breaking my back. My neck bones would vibrate into my ears. I knew it was resistance, but to what?

Resistance to merging, to love, to God, to reality, to dissolving, to oblivion?

Mind was awhirl and driving was the only sanity at hand. Howard Johnsons' along the turnpike became the waning assurance of a "real world."

It's all a game! *These others are acting for my sake, for everyone's sake. But in reality, there is really only me.*

Each person I run into is a messenger: the gas station attendant, the waitress at the lunch counter, they each enforce my panic by commenting with remarks like: *"It's a long way home alone. You need help?"* I get back in the car and I drive into the night.

My thoughts span the cosmos at light speed. I think every thought possible. Surely I was in the process of going insane, or was it "losing mind?"

I pull over when the pain is about to rip open my skull and spine. Lying there, I wait for oblivion. Some relief eventually comes and I drive on. Did these *others,* these anonymous silhouetted figures in the cars whizzing past, did they know that it's all going down the drain?

What am "I" supposed to do?

I had to *figure it out* somehow!

What am "I" supposed to do?

I get to a turnpike phone booth and somehow manage to dial collect. I called the only person in my confidence, my mother. I try not to frighten her. I know she will understand.

"You don't know how far down you are" was the auditory hallucination that I heard on the other end.

I ignore it, and go on to ask her to call my brother. I could no longer handle driving. He calls me back, and we arrange a place to meet.

He would get there as soon as he could. I was at another Howard Johnson Inn, off the Pennsylvania turnpike.

I get back to the car and try to sleep. It's still dark when I see them drive up. Grasping for reality, I run to them with flailing arms. To this day, I have never confessed to them my fearful dilemma. They knew enough to assume it had something to do with LSD. In the early dawn I am delivered to my mother and teenage sister's place.

> ### *What is a "flashback"?*
>
> Psychedelia likely borrowed the expression from movie editors, who borrowed it from the psychologists. It is essentially splicing a scene or situation from the past into a present real-time scene. But we are talking less about scenes and more about the apprehensions and replay of feelings. The best technical definition that I have found is as follows:
>
> *"The personal experiences that pop into your awareness, without any conscious, premeditated attempt to search and retrieve this memory."*
>
> —Flashback, wikipedia.com
>
> *In my own experience, I would emphasize the "pop," with its varied degree of urgency and determined defusing. The feeling is not merely a déjà vu sensation but, in mine and in other post-trip reports, a time-warp continuation of a session—picking up or flashing in where the original emotional occurrence left off.*
>
> *My flashback was very specific to an uncomfortable fearful feeling of familiarity with the great expanse of eternity; a fear of primordial struggle between expansion and contraction of the cosmos, and the accompanying Atlasian fear that I would drop the ball.*

There, too, I was unable to confess my story, I simply collapsed in exhaustion, and they let me rest. I must have been in sleep mode for days.

All her life my mother labored with the handicap of a leg brace and the increasing difficulty in walking as a result of childhood polio. My sister had long since taken over for me in helping my mother get around. In spite of her handicap my mother had considerable energy and enterprise, including most of the time as a single parent. Lucky for me, she was very intelligent, an entrepreneur in making a living for the family, an artist, and at that time a gifted and professional draftsman and architectural designer. But most importantly to my upbringing *(set)* was her transmission of *curiosity* and a spiritual outlook.

At times we marveled at the mysteries of life, and her own searching for the divine via the occult mystery schools, mysticism, and study in popular philosophy and world religions. All that, I presume, is why she never thought to call the men in white coats upon my insane arrival at her doorstep. She really had no idea what this latest page in my story was, which brought me there that morning. And I simply had no idea where to begin to tell her the story.

For the next few weeks, I maintained a precarious hold on reality, which I try to describe here.

Unbeknownst to my mother and sister, as I retreated in the apartment's makeshift cloistered setting, sleeping on the floor in the living room, the panic and painful bodily tension that had been triggered at Millbrook gave no indication of lessening. The painful tension along my spine and neck was unrelenting and continued day and night.

Daytime was spent in quiet company with my sister and mother, and both so concerned but caring enough to let me go at my own pace, and I doubt unaware that I was in silent agony, fear, and pain. But, of course, as far as I let them know, I was fine and thankful for a place to stay, away from what they could only presume was a traumatic experience which I had not explained.

Nights were spent in sleepless repetitive thought. And each time the *dilemma* would demand attention, the choice, I would desperately try to stop mind, obviously without success.

These first days at the apartment can be described as a continual shattering of body and mind, with no trace of spirit anywhere, only a constant state of pain and doubt—desperately, endlessly, trying to figure it out. Was it all to reveal some **impossible choice** that had no possible answer but fear?

If you were to ask me today, fifty years later, I would summarize my problem, my dilemma, my suffering, this way:

This was about how Consciousness conspires with mind to devise a way to get a message through from Consciousness to self at any risk, most particularly, at risk of losing mind, at risk of surrender of oneself. This was a **set-up**, *a forced dilemma—the biggest lesson that one can have in life. Somehow the reality of expansion vs contraction had become my personal problem, the ultimate question, a choice to be made with extinction either way. Whichever choice "I" made, for both myself and all egokind, God-hood & egohood had merged into a hellish responsibility to make the choice.*

One night lying there in the pain and dilemma with no particular intention or thought of remedy, I happened to turn toward a wall and a moonlit surface on a piece of furniture:

Suddenly a sense of presence.

At that instant, the pain vanished, replaced by utter relaxation and *bodily ecstasy*, infusing the room and mind to the limits of the cosmos. The *bliss* had returned, identical to that whole body experience in the LSD session, but as something being transmitted, not simply a given. I was surrendered, to what, or to whom, I was not sure, but absolutely trusting in that **presence**—a presence not unlike when a person enters the room. Only this was not an entity, nor person that I might name Lord or other.

This *presence* entered my cells, ignoring any separation between consciousness, mind, and body. It was felt as perfect equanimity at the body core.

If asked at the time, I would have verbalized it as an upward streaming shaft of sensual energy, a **possession** received as a presence that had full knowledge of me and what is on the other side of the cosmic abyss. It had returned to instruct me that all is perfect and there is no place to fall or fail.

All confusion was **surrendered** in that event[1] with head-to-heart bliss.

A release button had been pressed. But "I" had not pressed it. The *bliss* arrived most every night, just as I lay down to sleep. For the next decade or so my life revolved around further ecstatic episodes of various strengths and durations. Even as I thought the last episode had arrived, another would come, a month, a year, a decade later.

---

[1] This "surrender event" was unlike any ordinary "giving up;" it was spontaneous and uncaused.

A parable about "presence"

We can assume the narrator of this parable *(next column)* is fully aware of the wisdom tradition about *"presence;"* more importantly, [s]he also has *firsthand* experience of this *bliss or "shakti" part*.

The feeling observation is that there are two parallel aspects, making it difficult to separate the *"presence"* from *the idea of Kundalini*. The *Kundalini* part of the phrase *Kundalini-Shakti* refers to a goddess (Durga) and to her dormant form as having ringlets like the laying of clay in a pottery bowl, or the coiled sleeping posture of a serpent.

Shakti is said to be the feminine creative energy side of Shiva-Shakti, Shiva being the Consciousness *(or "presence")* within which the energy dance of Shakti (or bliss) occurs when the "serpent" is awakened or felt to arise in the body as bliss.

Once there was an inexperienced little fish who had the opportunity and courage to approach the Wisdom Fish, saying: "I have heard a lot of talk in my school about the **sea**, but what is the sea? Where is it?" The Elder Fish, astonished at the question, explains: "Well you live, move, and have your being in the sea. The sea is without and within, inside and outside of you. You are made in and of the sea and you will end in the sea. The sea is all that is around you, and you have been, are, and never will be separate from it as long as you live."

The wise Fish, seeing that the little fish is confused, then says, "When you know the sea, you will never gasp for water or be fearful of its depth."

We don't see what is all around us because it is "presence" It is what you are really never removed from.

Shiva Nataraja in the energy-dance of consciousness.

Kundalini-Shakti is described in technical vs. personal terms at the end of PartOne.

---

[2] At times the two are indistinguishable one from the other. See a limning of kundalini, pp.28-39.

This was tacit *instruction,*[1] this was *revelation,* not only in human ecstasy, but in how mind modifies reality to where illusions, beliefs, and habits, reflexively block such happiness. It even dawned on me that this bliss is always here, even if I do not feel it in the moment, in the circumstance. This was a message, a teaching, which I would identify much later as *Kundalini*—merely the energy of consciousness and reminder of non-separation from the divine.

I was at the apartment for several weeks, then realized I'd better try to get my job back at the ad agency and look for a place to live. Luckily, even after my discourteous resignation, they gave me my job back. My boss welcomed me without the least inquiry as to what I had been up to. I myself had no explanation of what I was up to, nor why I had become caught in egohood at the expense of *Godhood.*

Presence, surrender, and *ecstasy* would describe my Godhood triad. Yet, no two events were alike in character or intensity, and sometimes one part, but not the other two parts would arise. Over time, I tried tacitly logging what conditions or attitudes of the day might impact the character of that night's episode. To this day, I have not *figured out* what conditions, if any, are necessary for a visitation of this *inexplicable energy of consciousness.* When this was received, it was not in the traditional lotus sitting position, rather lying on my stomach or flat on my back. I began to understand the idea of *grace,* not in the religious sense, but simply *a gift,* unearned by any action or condition on my part. Gratitude was my constant mood.

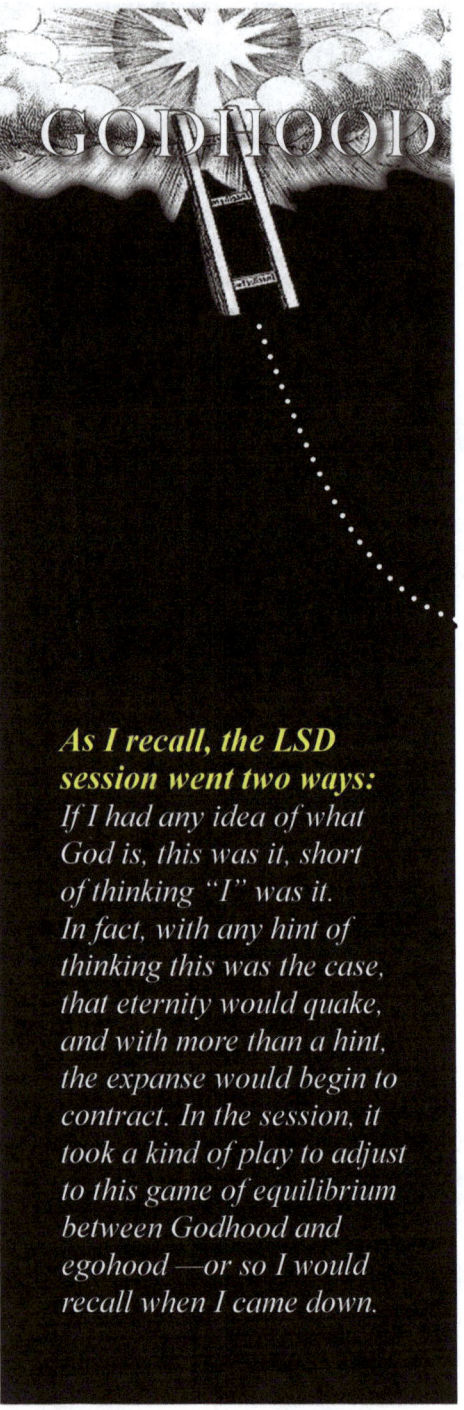

As I recall, the LSD session went two ways:
If I had any idea of what God is, this was it, short of thinking "I" was it. In fact, with any hint of thinking this was the case, that eternity would quake, and with more than a hint, the expanse would begin to contract. In the session, it took a kind of play to adjust to this game of equilibrium between Godhood and egohood —or so I would recall when I came down.

---

[1] This feeling of tacit "instruction" would be confirmed as the "work" went on, p. 38.

No limit, no up or down. Actually, at the height of the LSD session itself, there was no thought in that eternity, only stark being, a complete knowing as not knowing. All was obvious, whatever I was, I was all there is, extended to and beyond everything and anything possibly existing. There was no limit, no edge, all space and time was there, all possible bliss, and no want for more.

It now had been a few months after the episode at Millbrook sent me down that *road of oblivion*. Back at work, and while still in the freshness and transformation of my consciousness, I also experienced a profound transformation of body. I had previously been a fingernail biting, pack-a-day smoker, and occasional drinker, somewhat a requirement when working in an ad agency. Over the months and without will power or withdrawal, I spontaneously quit coffee, smoking, and alcohol—the body could not tolerate these substances.

Between the ecstatic episodes at night and a few that started to happen at work, I was a functional nervous wreck. There was still a considerable background tension. The dilemma was not fully resolved. I would lock myself in the ad agency mensroom and lie down on the cold tile floor, in fetal position, to relieve the painful resisting stress in my back and neck. A polarity of emotional states became my daily experience. Yet, a **wisdom, of sort, developed** from pondering my existential state and being instructed by Kundalini-Shakti.

When I say *"instructed,"* there was no entity, no teacher, but rather a healing rest in unknowing, unlearning, an indifference to what mind thought it knew, and a repeated surrender to the body, the feeling, the presence, which seemed to know more about what to do than "I" or mind. There was no choice but to listen to and follow the body. **Synchronicity** and **premonition** became a regular thing, if not a normal occurrence.

The flow of mind was observed in a new way, a *"feeling way,"* a *"feeling observation,"* and I would later describe it as an *interruption,* or *gap,* or **"nullpoint"**[2] in the flow of mind.

---

[1] As time went on, this "nullpoint" would prove to be the code-breaker in the "work," *PartThree*.

Finally, almost a decade after having taken LSD, my existential dilemma of Godhood vs. egohood, which I began to call *"the mistake of identity,"* came to a sudden and graceful end. The error was not realized on my own, rather from what I read in *Cutting Through Spiritual Materialism*, the book by Chögyam Trungpa—a most simple explanation of my fall from expansive bliss, that I felt at the height of the LSD session, to the agony there at the end in coming down.

There in a couple of pages, was my dilemma described 180 degrees from what I had otherwise held as the reality of the matter. I have since been able to frame it in the form of a three part existential question:

If there is only one being, am I it? Is this Godhood or Egohood? And if this was all a COSMIC JOKE, what was the PUNCH LINE?

Trungpa may not himself have framed it as *"the cosmic joke,"* but judge for yourself whether he does indeed cut through to the core, to the *punch line* of what I thought was my own exclusive spiritual dilemma or *mistake of identifying* with God, without Trungpa calling it any more than the ego-life-experience.

Such is a common mistake according to his paraphrasing of *The Abhidhamma*[1] scripture of Theravada Buddhism *(see panel, pg 34),* which is the source text from which Trungpa paraphrases what seems to be the *"message"* that I most needed, but least expected, to hear—a message that exemplifies our predisposed mind SET in light of the psychedelic and materialistic (dualistic) approach to *Godhood*.

CUTTING THROUGH MY DILEMMA

1973
CUTTING THROUGH SPIRITUAL MATERIALISM

The author, Chögyam Trungpa Rinpoche, had followed the Dalai Lama out of Tibet and himself became a preeminent teacher of several brands of Buddhism in the West. He relinquished his monkhood shortly after arriving in the West to write extensively. He eventually founded the Naropa University in Boulder, Colorado in 1974.

Credit for quotes on pages 118-119, *Cutting Through Spiritual Materialism*, by Chögyam Trungpa, © 1984, Reprinted by arrangement with The Permissions Company, Inc. on behalf of Shambhala Publications Inc., www.shambhala.com.

Chögyam Trungpa Rinpoche 1939-1987

---

[1] See panel, p26.

THIS READING REPRESENTS THE MESSAGE AND EXPLANATION OF MY DILEMMA.

The Joke

"The beginning point is that there is open space, belonging to no one.

... It is like a spacious hall where there is room to dance about, where there is no danger of knocking things over or tripping over things,

*... We **are** this space, we are **one** with it, with... intelligence, and openness...*

Because it is spacious, it brings inspiration to dance about, ...we begin to spin more than necessary to express the space. At this point we become self-conscious, conscious that 'I' am [God] dancing in the space.

The monkey [the "I"] dwells upon the idea of limitless space. [S]he watches limitless space, [s]he is here and limitless space is there and [s]he watches it. [S]he feeds him[or her]self with this [Godhood bliss] experience ...[S]he also dwells upon the intelligence which perceives that limitless space.

So ego watches limitless space and consciousness from its central headquarters. The empire of ego is completely extended. Even the central authority cannot imagine how far its territory extends... it includes everything."[2]

The Punch Line

"At such a point, space is no longer space as such. It becomes solid. Instead of being one with the space, we feel solid space as a separate entity, as tangible. This is the first experience of duality–space and I. I am dancing in space, and this spaciousness is a solid, separate thing. Duality means 'space and I,' rather than being completely one with the space. This is the birth of 'form,' of 'other' [The embryonic sack].

The monkey has managed [by way of this entheogen] to reach the ultimate level of achievement, but [s]he has not transcended the dualistic logic upon which achievement depends. The walls of the monkey's house still have the quality of 'other' in a subtle sense. The monkey may have achieved a temporary harmony and peace and bliss through a seeming union with [its] projections, but the whole thing is subtly fixed. The monkey thinks that [s]he has achieved nirvana [Godhood], but actually [s]he has achieved only a temporary state of Egohood.

Sooner or later the absorption [bliss] wears off and the monkey begins to panic and gets preoccupied with figuring out what has gone wrong."[3]

Thus, my preoccupation with the "dilemma" was finally ended.

---

[2]Trungpa, *Cutting Through Spiritual Materialism*, pp123-124. [3] Ibid, pp143-145 [My brackets]

Even if way back there, in the good company of Tim Leary, had I cut through my fear to tell him my suffering of *"The Cosmic Joke,"* I doubt if he or anyone else could have delivered the *punch line:* **the mistake of identity** more clearly than Trungpa's answer *(previous page)*. And if after that reading, it is not all that clear to you, either in importance or in message, perhaps the following highlighted comparisons will help. *(Trungpa's message is in italic.)*

"The monkey thinks that [s]he has achieved nirvana [Godhood], but actually [s]he has achieved only a temporary state of Egohood." [My brackets]

Trungpa's dharmic explanation nicely cuts up my LSD session into three easy pieces:

Piece 1: From my first-person view, I certainly had identified with *"Nirvanic Bliss,"* Godhood, *"limitless space and consciousness,"* the only one.

Piece 2: The "vanishing of the *"Nirvanic Bliss"* had become *my fault*—*"what has gone wrong?"*

Piece 3: Post session thinking that I was the only being and periodic panicked flashbacks in which that one had to make a choice: **either eternal contraction or eternal expansion of the universe, the cosmos, the world, reality itself.** Yet, I always blocked it, never making a choice—for both seemed to mean annihilation. And *"preoccupied with figuring out what has gone wrong."*

"The monkey [ego] has managed [by way of a psychedelic] to reach the ultimate level of achievement, but [s]he has not transcended the dualistic logic upon which achievement depends."
[My brackets]

The Abhidhamma, which is what Trungpa is paraphrasing, was a Pali language text unique to Theravada school of Buddhism. Its methodology looks at things in terms of occasions or events instead of sequences or processes. The *Abhidhammapitaka* is the last of three text groupings (*pitakas*) written around 200 years after the death of the Buddha.[1]

The monkey is the metaphor used as the stand-in for the ego, egohood, or the I am, the I, as it apparently develops and achieves *illusory status and, in fact, false entity (see below)* through time and all manner of phenomena in the space of Egohood—*"the empty house where the captive monkey resides."*

The I am [It]: "Actually there is no such thing as 'I am;' it is the product of the intellect which says, 'Let's give it a name, let's call it something, let's call it 'I am.' 'I' is the label which unifies into one whole the disorganized and scattered development of ego.

In a sense, it might be said that primordial intelligence is operating all the time, but it is being employed by dualistic fixation. In the beginning stages of the development of ego this intelligence operates as the intuitive sharpness of feeling. Later it operates in the form of intellect [mind]." [2]

---

[1] en.wikipedia.org/wiki/Abhidamma_Pitaka.   [2] Trungpa, Ibid, pp127-128. [My brackets].

> *"The monkey may have achieved a temporary harmony and peace and bliss through a seeming union with [its] projections, but the whole thing is subtly fixed."*[1]

Here, even ego can appreciate that ego cannot be transcended to where, however *"subtly fixed,"* there is not some trace of paradoxical *dualistic logic,* since merely thinking *(you are God)* creates an experiencer, the thinker, the thinking. I know that some, including myself, are tempted to use the expression *"non dual experience"* in regard to one like mine—my objection is that it is still from *egohood* (from duality) that the experiencer, the "I" is making that call.

The renowned Hindu yogi Ramana Maharshi said: *"Even a [temporary] state of **Samadhi** is a state of mind."* So, as I understand Trungpa's dharma: it is not by any thought, even in thinking *"I am God,"* or *"We are all God,"* that God is realized. And in the same way, no "thought" about reality is reality, be it thought of its annihilation or continuance. *Reality* remains *What Is.*

All this is an unnecessary paradox, which would not be such, were it not for the human *idea* of Godhood & Egohood which optimizes:

> *"... the dualistic logic upon which achievement [of such notions] depends."*

In contrast to my mistake of identity all those years, and with the help of Alan Watts' admonition to do the integrating *work,* and Trungpa's explanation of my existential dilemma, I now try to practice a *novel mode* of thinking toward repurposing mind *(PartThree).*

That practice is an ongoing thought experiment, explained in *PartTwo,* and technicality applied in *PartThree*—all with the prerequisite understanding that the reader is expected to partially glean from *PartOne,* and the whole mistake of "identification" of a "self" and "other" in the flow of consciousness called mind or ... *"the monkey":*

> *"The monkey needs to develop panoramic awareness and transcendental knowledge. Panoramic awareness allows the monkey to see the space [sphere] in which the struggle occurs so that [s]he can begin to see its ironical and humorous quality. [S]he laughs through the hallucination. ...The clarity and precision of transcendental knowledge allows the monkey to see the walls [of its house] in a different way.]S]he begins to realize that the world was never outside of him [or her] self, that it was [their] own dualistic attitude, **the separation of "I" and "other,"** that created the problem."* [2]

That *"separation of 'I' and "other,"* not only *"created"* my dilemma, my own personal crisis, but more important to the theme of this book, it created the global crisis, all crises. And, more than an *"attitude,"* that *"separation"* is the ultimate illusion or hallucination, all of which has a phenomenological explanation that will be explored step-by-step, in *PartTwo* of this book.

In the meantime and to conclude this backstory to all of that, it seems necessary to give the reader a full account, or explanation, of what I came to call Kundalini-Shakti—that *bliss* presence of the *energy of consciousness,* which was my mystic/consort for so many years.

---

[1]Trungpa [My brackets]. [2]Trungpa, C.S.M., pp146,147 [My brackets].

At the time of its arrival, and for a year or so thereafter, I had no idea that the bliss I was experiencing was called Kundalini-Shakti. My name for it was simply the *"presence (of) bliss,"* somehow coincident with *"surrender"* (As described on page 20) .

As I recall, it was at work one day that I had a disturbing reaction while turning to a colorful article, in my favorite art magazine, about Hindu tantric art showing "chakras" or centers along the spine, with the word Kundalini in the text. Suddenly I felt a thud in my tail bone or perineum. This was the first suspicion that what I had been experiencing was called "Kundalini-Shakti."

It seems there was a subtle revival of interest in Hindu tantra in the late 1960's and quickly had become a topic of media interest. I suspected it had everything to do with the emerging use of psychedelics, including my own. Yet, since the article had disturbed me, I hesitated doing any investigation into the matter for the next several years.

It was not until 1975 that I had overcome the "shattering" or trauma of my experience, enough to put a few notes on paper, which these decades later has supplied the source text for this narration of my experience.

When I did finally look into what others had to say about Kundalini, there was no internet, only brick & mortar libraries. So the research took years. Books classified under schools of yoga in the Hindu tradition were rare. Western appropriation of Eastern yoga is casual, used as a body fitness regimen, with no anticipation or even knowledge of Kundalini. And even today, with the internet, an authentic description and practice of *Kundalini yoga* is a rare find.

What I find most surprising today is that out of the scarce psychedelic literature of decades ago and in all of it today there is only obscure linking of psychedelics with Kundalini, and nothing about it lasting for any extended period of time after a psychedelic session, long after any psychoactive substance can be found in the body/brain chemistry.

The first thing I tried to find out was had there ever been linkage. How would a yoga lineage come to practice something so esoteric as Kundalini Yoga, without someone at the start of the lineage having taken psychedelics?

But I quickly found that question difficult to answer looking at it from the present teaching of lineages professing Kundalini as a so-called practice or yoga. So the next question was how did my experience compare to what is being described using the term Kundalini-Yoga? Was there any benefit in my *"learning"* something that had already been given spontaneously?

I began with various Western writers, such as Carl Jung's 1932 lectures on Kundalini and Sir John Woodroffe, aka Arthur Avalon's series of books on ancient Hindu tantra published in the 1920's. It seemed I was coming across a simple parroting of teachings that had long since lost any resemblance to what might be instructive, or any real discussion of what Kundalini is and what the spectrum of its characteristics are. These were Western writers who translated these texts, adding their own Western bias. I then found Eastern writers who, with few exceptions, likewise were simply parroting dogma and copying ritual and iconography.

THIS PANEL HOLDS A GLIMPSE OF HINDU TANTRIC TRADITION AROUND KUNDALINI

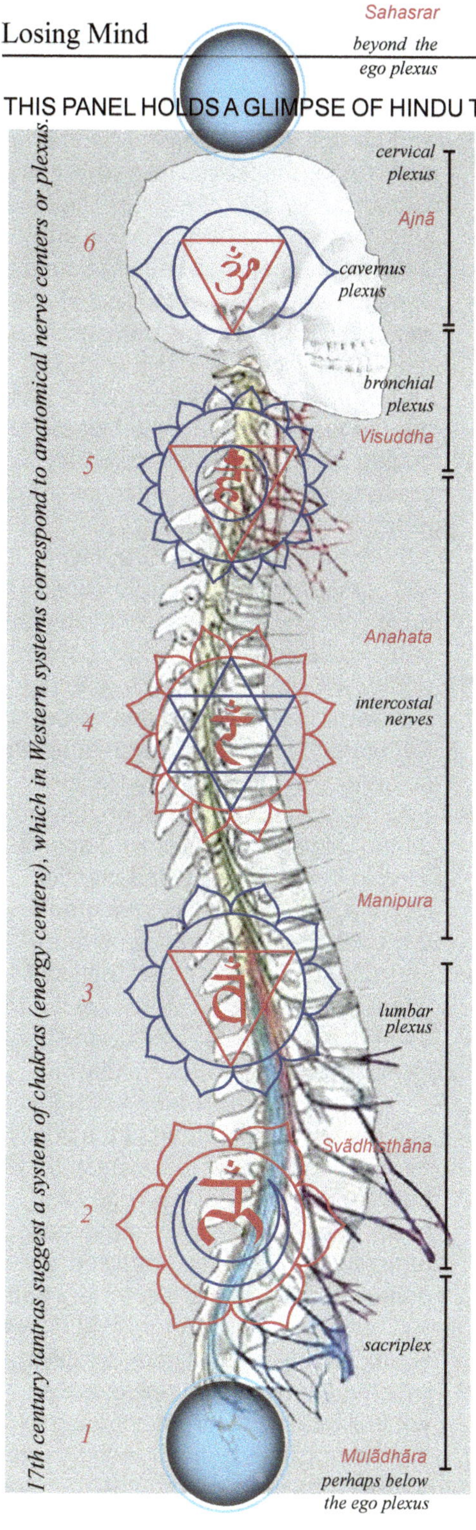
Sahasrar
beyond the ego plexus
17th century tantras suggest a system of chakras (energy centers), which in Western systems correspond to anatomical nerve centers or plexus.¹
cervical plexus
Ajnã
6
cavernus plexus
bronchial plexus
Visuddha
5
Anahata
intercostal nerves
4
Manipura
3
lumbar plexus
Svãdhisthãna
2
sacriplex
1
Mulãdhãra
perhaps below the ego plexus

7
6
5
4

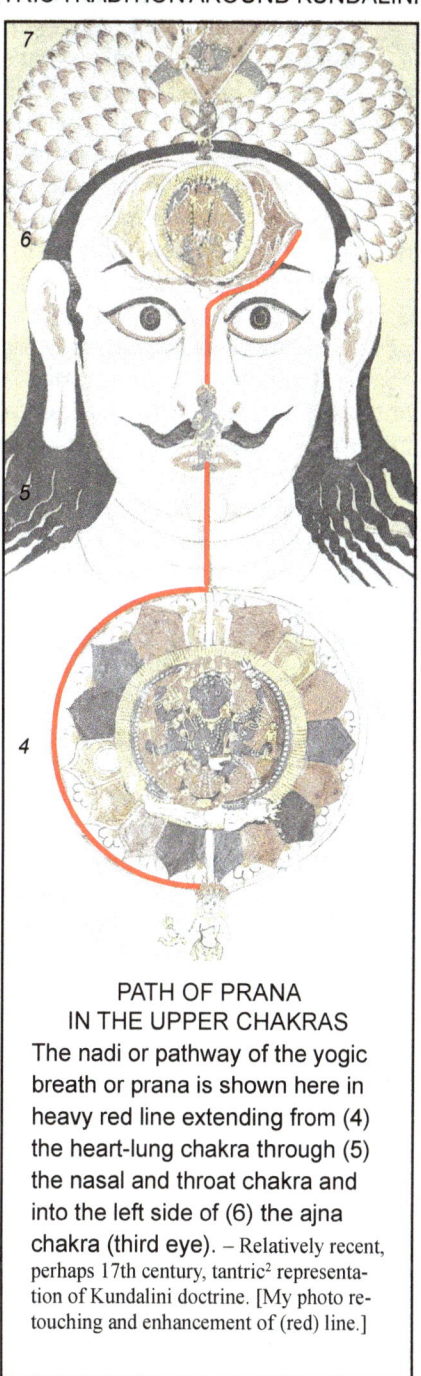

PATH OF PRANA
IN THE UPPER CHAKRAS

The nadi or pathway of the yogic breath or prana is shown here in heavy red line extending from (4) the heart-lung chakra through (5) the nasal and throat chakra and into the left side of (6) the ajna chakra (third eye). – Relatively recent, perhaps 17th century, tantric[2] representation of Kundalini doctrine. [My photo retouching and enhancement of (red) line.]

[1] Left column: Artist's composite of tantra symbols and names for the chakras parallel to anatomical nerve plexus regions. [2] Tantra or tantric: "tan" (Skt) a "weave: of teachings techniques or practice.

Although the ancient Hindu tantric tradition claims exclusive knowledge of these so-called maps of consciousness *(previous panel)*, the symbolism here has been a grab bag for many interpretations, that even Hindu scholars (tantrics) have misinterpreted.

Taking a less dogmatic, more secular or generic approach to mapping the so-called *secret anatomy* of Kundalini-Shakti, I show *(next panel)* the skinless physiology of the body in the Hatha yoga *cobra pose (Bhujangasana)*. This hatha yoga asana is the first spontaneous pose I experienced, trying to cope with kriyas or inherent stress of resistance to Kundalini-Shakti possession.

In my own case, the traditional outline of energy centers seemed to be of little importance. The more intuitive feeling was simply: **A frontal (down) and spinal (up) current of consciousness.**

The *next panel* bypasses traditional Hindu iconography, lotus petals, and Sanskrit seed syllables, keeping the whole discussion in a phenomenological, rather than religious vein.

Note the number key: (**6**) the ajna door or third eye, reportedly just behind the brow of the skull bone, (**5**) the nasal/throat chakra said to connect mind with heart, and (**4**) the heart chakra, just behind the breast bone, with its horizontal tripartite nodes. It is perhaps (**4**) the heart chakra that can be considered the fulcrum or median of an axis extending both vertically and horizontally to infinity, with (**3**) the soft solar plexus bellows or *prana* (breath) thrusting the Shakti energy through the hollow nadi *"sushummai"* channel in the center of the spinal cord, connecting all chakras, including (**2**) the plexus of genitalia where our sex is pleasurably felt.

Number keys **1** & **7** locate pole and portals to this secret structure, and seem to be the least explored in this extraordinary axis of feeling. They are said, by the Hindu adept, to be entry way to the most profound bliss states of mind called the *"samadhis."* These two, 1 & 7 chakras, are also said to be respectively located infinitely above and slightly below the body core, with the *"sahasrar"* (**7**) being the highest chakra, and said to be known only by grace to the yogi or yogini most surrendered into this yoga (union).

Even in the late 1980's, I was still comparing my Kundalini experience with any literary descriptions, and came to personally know two contemporary writers considered experts on Kundalini: Lee Sannella and Georg Feuerstein. Lee was a psychiatrist and cofounder of the Kundalini Clinic in San Francisco. Georg Feuerstein was an Indologist (Indian Studies) specializing in the philosophy and practice of Yoga, with 20 books to his credit. We each happened to belong to a group that often presented topics of philosophical interest. At one of these gatherings, both men offered to speak together on the topic of Kundalini.

In the Q&A after their scholarly talk I asked if either man had actually experienced Kundalini, to which they both replied that they had not. I received their answer with unexpressed amazement. But later, I realized, it's quite common that an expert in a subject, or even your own family M.D., will speak to your complaint or condition, which they have never experienced, yet feel qualified to treat acording to their medical bias, rather than based on your particular report.

Kundalini as a name for Shakti (feminine side of Shiva) and as the evolutionary energy of consciousness in the body, appears as a technical term in Tantrism and Shaktism as early as the 11th century, and later Kundalini is adopted as a technical term in Hatha yoga in the 15th century and becomes widely used in the Yoga teachings by the 16th century. The phrase "serpent power" was coined by Sir John Woodroffe who published translations of two 16th-century treatises on laya yoga (Kundalini yoga) in 1919. *"When Kundalini Shakti is conceived as a goddess, then, when it rises to the head, it unites with the Supreme Being (Lord Shiva). Then the aspirant is said to become engrossed in infinite bliss."*

Although chakras per se were not my direct experience, they seem useful navigation buoys on a map of infinite consciousness.

Regardless of the trigger, be it yoga, meditation, or an entheogenic session, once the body is feelingly awakened to the bliss at its core, neither body nor mind seems to have a choice but to surrender to that current. For me, reflexive resistance took its painful toll for almost a year. When *the "I"* was eventually surrendered, the body instantly followed; then it was the body that instructed mind in ascent and descent to the heart of that yoga.

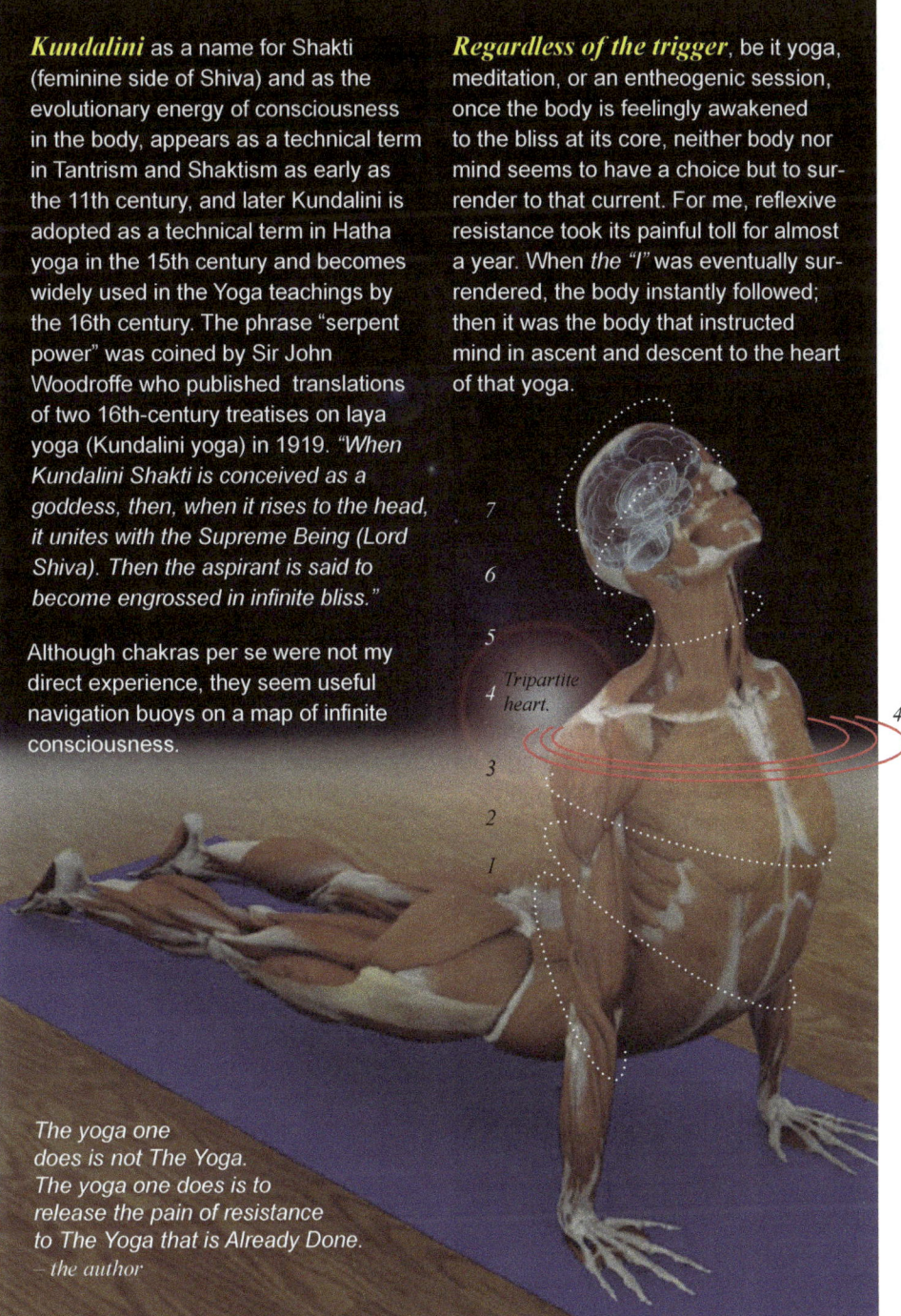

Tripartite heart.

The yoga one does is not The Yoga. The yoga one does is to release the pain of resistance to The Yoga that is Already Done.
—*the author*

Image © C. Macivor & R. Long, MD / BandhaYoga (Author added circles & numbers to original.)

Let's get back to my actual report: What I am calling Kundalini-Shakti is difficult, if not impossible, to describe. Putting aside, for the moment, the Kriyas, pain and mental resistance to its free flow, the pleasurable side of the experience could be described as 10,000 degrees more in duration and intensity than orgasm. And compared to the same energy of consciousness, whole bodily felt in the LSD session, add at least 100,000 degrees intensity and duration. However, even comparing this ethereal or subtle bliss with the pleasure of orgasm is where the esoteric aspect gets lost on an exoteric culture. It is easy to imagine how any pleasure producing pathway can be abused, diminished, and/or become destructive to both spirit and body.

Most Western appropriation of yoga is casual, used as a body fitness regimen, with no anticipation, or even knowledge, of Kundalini. But with the internet, *Kundalini yoga* studios and ashrams have become a common business enterprise. The usual warning: "Consumer beware" might often apply.

Perhaps not in popular literature, but if my case is any example, there should be at least a small percentage of the psychedelic culture where Kundalini or the word "bliss" has showed up in trip reports and or in follow-up reports.

What tacit instruction I did receive from Kundalini-Shakti's *presence* and pass on to you here, I credit not to any persistence on the ego "I's" part, rather to a mutual devotion. Part of that instruction is that, however profound the bliss and feeling of ascent, none of it is more than having won some karmic lottery, unless you "get the message" and do the "work" between episodes.

Like most of us, I have no answer to the *"Hard Problem"* of how the apparent *"self"* is fitted to the body. Upon awakening from sleep, like you, I feelingly arrive in a skin, remarkably like the membrane of a cell, devised over 3.5 billion years ago, to protect and separate *self* from *other*. As for any primal feeling connection to the energy of consciousness, we are normally unaware of any.

But, otherwise I am talking about Kundalini as an open or closed-eyes visual and *feeling encounter* with an indescribably intimate energy. After some extended experience with it, episodes might arise shortly after a premonition of its penetration at the arch of the back just below the rib cage, or from a mere brush of the knee or elbow against a garment. Once there, close your eyes and simply surrender into it! For me there was a visual field, usually a deep black, awaiting shapes, constellations of color particles, gossamer waves, in any visual or sensual configuration you can imagine.

If what descriptions I manage to put into words, or you manage to put into words, do not agree with the experience you have had, or may yet have, I leave it to the discerning reader to take what is useful and never mind the rest.

As I said, Kundalini is part bliss and part intimate instruction, a telling without words. When I listen carefully, the message extends far beyond discrete chakras in vertebrate bodies with human brains, as if to inform me that its apparent symmetry of seven nodes or chakras is a universal structure—a symmetry of the nature and structure of all that we imagine is mind and/or body, cosmos or home planet. When you look for it, that *septenary symmetry* is everywhere.

THIS PANEL HOLDS THE BEGINNINGS OF A SCIENCE NEEDED AROUND KUNDALINI

A renowned Indian surgeon takes us on a quick tour of Western Anatomy by way of the nadis or channels of Kundalini-Shakti:

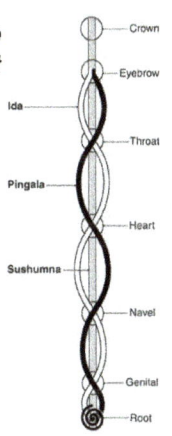

"When we study the construction, location and function of the Spinal Cord and the Sushumna Nadi, we can readily say that the Spinal Cord was called Sushumna Nadi by the yogis. The Western Anatomy deals with the gross form and functions of the Spinal Cord, while the Yogins of ancient times dealt with all about the subtle (Sukshma) nature.

Sushumna Nadi passes through the hollow cylindrical cavity of the vertebral column. The spinal cord is not divided or separated from the brain. It is continuous with the brain. All the cranial and spinal nerves are connected with this cord. The spinal cord opens out into the fourth ventricle of the brain in the medulla oblongata. From the fourth ventricle it runs along the third, then the fifth ventricle of the brain and finally it reaches the crown of the head, Sahasrara Chakra.

Sushumna extends from the Muladhara Chakra (second vertebra of coccygeal region) to Brahmarandhra. The Western Anatomy admits that there is a central canal in the Spinal Cord, called Canalis Centralis and that the cord is made up of grey and white brain-matter. The spinal Cord is ... suspended in the hollow of the spinal column.

Within this Sushumna there is a very fine minute canal ...This canal is known as Brahmanadi through which Kundalini, when awakened, passes from Muladhara to Sahasrara Chakra. In this centre exist all the six Chakras (Muladhara, Svadhishthana, Manipura, Anahata, Vishuddha and Ajna). ...The lower extremity of the Chitra Nadi is called Brahmadvara, the door of Brahman, as Kundalini has to pass through this door to Brahmarandhra. In a general sense the Sushumna Nadi itself (gross Spinal Cord) is called Brahma Nadi because Brahma Nadi is within the Sushumna.

The Ida and Pingala Nadis are on the left and right sides of the spine. ...When the Nadis are full of impurities, the breath cannot pass into the middle Nadi. So one should practice Pranayama for the purification of Nadis.

The Muladhara Chakra is located at the base of the spinal column. ...It is just below the Kanda and the junction where Ida, Pingala and Sushumna Nadis meet ...where the Muladhara Chakra is situated. This is the Adhara Chakra (support) as the other Chakras are above this... Here Kundalini lies dormant."

—Source: http://drpaulose.com, from an 2010 article by Dr. K. O. Paulose, FRCS, DLO, Consulting ENT associated with Jubilee Memorial Hospital, Palayam Thiruvananthapuram, India.

I will speak directly to that septenary symmetry in *PartTwo*. However, while here, in Kundalini-Shakti's pleasurable embrace, there is no thinking, **no need**, wish, or desire to explain its consuming *possession*. But then as narrator of the story, I have to consider the general reader—seriously or perhaps only casually seeking information.

Therefore, I will include here more of my personal history with Kundalini and what you can expect if and when this energy might become the overwhelming aspect of your daily experience. I feel it important in the long run to give a heads-up about the **downside as well as the upside** (so to speak) to having Kundalini-Shakti in your life.

For example: Between occasions of this indescribable intimacy one might fearfully begin to obsess on the questions: "Am I crazy? Is this divine or egoic possession? Why me?" And by this point, I hope it is clear that the Kundalini experience and the psychedelic (or entheogenic) experience are not necessarily synonymous, One can happen without the other, although in the phenomenological sense these are both *mind-manifesting* events.

Whereas, *entheogenic-mind* is more the explosion or loss of mind, Kundalini-Shakti takes the *trajectory* of an arrow to an unknown target. And because both have to do with *"bliss,"* they can be put either into the Western bias in favor of the *"Divine Realm"* or in the Eastern bias of Vedanta Advaita's *"Unconditional Realm"* or in the Buddhist's *Dharmakaya*. And to add one more disclaimer, none of this conversation is to be construed as advocacy either for or against the use of psychoactive substance or doing a yoga practice.

With Kundalini, I felt a more tolerable bliss-field than in the entheogenic experience. From onset to finish of an ascent or descent in a typical 90 minute episode, there was an awareness of real time but not real motion, although the trajectory could be imagined to be as deep and as wide as the cosmos.

With my eyes closed, a visual field of anything I wished to imagine against a pixilated matrix, from a sparkling stellar night sky to a gossamer spectrum of colorful particles in an upward circular flow. In the early years, it was all I could do to take-it-all-in. Later, I experimented by trying to steer the flow, only to discover a discomfort in doing so, and a quicker, even screeching halt to the ride. Yet, the urge to steer, to manipulate, seemed permitted. I simply had no idea where or how to aim the flow, even with all manner of experimentation over the months and years. I simply let it take the lead and tried to keep up.

I have come to liken the *Kundalini body (anatomy)* to a butterfly, which obviously has nothing to do with its appearance or design and beautiful colored accoutrements. As for who or what did have something to do with the apparent *latent* or cocoon vehicle from which the Shakti springs, we might look closer *(panel)* at what Biologists and Anatomists have called *"embryonic recapitulation."* Whatever we might find that are the forces behind the source and purpose of Kundalini, I have come to think of those forces at work from both ends of the evolutionary paradigm, allowing for obsolescence of the duality-experience while at the same time having provided a latent structure in the 3.5 billion year old tree of life for the *Kundalini-presence* to reside.

The future as well as the primal expression of the evolutionary energy of consciousness is a question worth considering:

Tantrics describe Kundalini as a primal energy, remaining dormant or in stasis, like a snake coiled in sleep in the deepest core of our secret anatomy and say that only a few will feel this energy activated in their lifetime. This idea of *latency* cannot be overlooked if we are to ever begin to understand the phenomenon in light of any developing science of Kundalini and/or psychedelics.

Looking at discoveries already evident in classic biology, such as *embryonic recapitulation* and the discoveries emerging from the new *quantum biology,* perhaps we can expect real answers to what role Kundalini plays in the evolution of our species. If we start with the *latency* question, might that also suggest that the embryonic stages that show molecular features of ancestral or primal organisms (i.e. gills and tail recapitulation) might also include latent neuro-structures primed for present and future use? I realize that within biology, recapitulation is merely a sidenote; however, in the broader view of cognitive development, it is a serious consideration.

The few scientists who are studying Kundalini may disagree at times; that is how science works. But I also expect that as we have seen with the latest neuroimaging techniques, facinating discoveries in the last five years outshine those of the last fifty. Consider this common thread in reports of both entheogenic and Kundalini experiences: the "I" becomes an obsolete construct and impairment to the otherwise more expansive mode of mind and presence of consciousness. And the fact that both Kundalini and entheogens disrupt the *self/other* or *default mode* of mind demonstrates first: *a purpose* for the existence of Kundalini and second: how it fits in the scheme of the continued evolutionary advancement of the human species. Obviously, the capability to function and thrive in new realms of consciousness has been the history of the human species since the cognitive leaps in our consciousness from homo erectus to homo sapiens. Sooner or later, and very likely much sooner than we can imagine, Kundalini may be a common experience.

©2016 Art of kundalini [not silhouette] licensed from Samuel Farrand, www.SamuelFarhand.com

In admiring the butterfly's wings, it is worth a heads-up on a few ancillary affects to watch for. I mentioned a tendency to try steering the Kundalini. At times it was a desire to reach a climax, but not at all the same as the tendency experienced in sexual activity.

There is no direct sexual component, yet one could *turn it* or make it so if one wished to settle for orgasm rather than bliss. If there is a pre-climactic component, it is a cumulative pressure to mentally push at the so-called ajna (door) chakra or what I feelingly-observed just behind the center of the brow, and the impulse to *push* in toward the top of the inside of the skull, a push to the degree of discomfort, and never completed by me as an accomplished climax.

In off moments, pressure from below, and perhaps in compensation for not reaching a climactic state at higher levels of Kundalini, however blissful, would lead me to succumb to ejaculation. It may be this led to fewer visits of the consort Kundalini. I have the strong hunch that yogis and yogins more practiced than I, have discovered that **Brahmacharya** (abstinence) sustains, even increases, the Kundalini episodes.

There is definitely a feeling of ethereal purity and a devotional ambiance surrounding an affair with the consort Kundalini-Shakti. [S]he is a taskmaster, not to be trifled with or cheated.

I also confess in those first years to never having meditated, as I understand the term today. I sat on the meditation cushion for hours without a trace of Kundalini. The affair with my consort was always in lying down with her, allowing passionate breath (hyperventilation) to kindle sparks into those flames of possession and bliss.

However, over time, the secret breath often failed to light the necessary fire. I learned quickly that egoic (self) effort was fruitless; there had to first be some greater degree of spontaneity and or non-mindful surrender before the sparks became bliss.

The breath *(Prana)* and breathing aspect in Kundalini is especially integral to the whole event or episode of shakti or energy flow felt both visually and tactually in body and mind. At times my lungs and heart expanded with each breath and seemed to be driven beyond any previous capacity or volume. With eyes closed, lying there, I expanded to cosmic proportions, and in kundalini's embrace it seemed like a breathing intercourse with the cosmos—a kind of *yab-yum*[1] expanding outward into all of space—the breath of the cosmos. Also, at times, after exhalation there seemed to be no reason to inhale again, time stood still, until the next breath, effortlessly, finally, arrived.

I can also report several, perhaps four, distinct forms, if not **levels or degrees of Kundalini bliss**: I mentioned the whole-mind, whole-body version in the midst of the entheogenic experience. The second is specific to the heart area, as the *presence or love bliss*. The third is the experience in the respiratory and head chakras. And the fourth is experienced in the limbs, upper thigh, groin area, as well as in the hands and feet. The feeling in the heart seems to take a horizontal rather than vertical path. It all may be happening in the same transcendent matrix of energy, but these are distinctions that may be of guidance in getting your bearings in regard to your own story and the traditional reports of such states of body and mind.

---

[1]Yab-yum: divine intimacy, fusing masculine  and feminine (Shiva-Shakti) energies.

THE AUTHOR'S DEPICTION OF THE FEELING-OBSERVATION OF KUNDALINI-SHAKTI.

Art by the author ©1985, 2023, Vertical (3-7) and horizontal *** envisioned energy of consciousness.

I say states of "mind" rather than states of "consciousness" to indicate the intuition that there is Consciousness (with a capital "C") that stands undisturbed, unmodified (surrender itself), beyond the body just as mind stands beyond the brain. And when I say "I lost my mind," perhaps better said: "I" was somehow surrendered out of mind into that "C" of Consciousness.

Earlier in this story I emphasized that Kundalini seemed to have two dimensions, **bliss** and **instruction**. These stood out among its other characteristics. And here, many years since that tacit instruction, I came across a short video talk by someone, who appears to be adept in the school of kundalini-yoga, explain in plain English my intuition of receiving tacit *instruction:*

"There are three forms of Kundalini: Chit-Kundalini is the form in which all energy is understood to be **information** *(knowledge). And knowledge itself aggregates as cognitive process. Prana-Kundalini is the aggregations of cognitive process into material and physiological form, and function."*

—Excerpt from a 2018 talk by Swami Chetanananda

That's good news, so I really was receiving *instruction* between the lines of bliss. It would have been nice, back then, to have heard that confirmation. Yet he even went on in the video to explain something that astonished and informed me even more. Again, in plain language, he seemingly outlined, in a single paragraph, the whole of what I have written down, in detail, in the next part of this book *(PartTwo)*, which is, as I see it now, all about how Kundalini manifests as information or word:

"Originally [primordially], Kundalini was simply that dimension in which energy becomes knowledge and knowledge [information] becomes sound and sound becomes letters and letters [seed syllables] become words and words [language] completely influence how our brain [or mind] perceives the environment [world] in which we live."

—Ibid. Brackets are [my own words]

In other words this is how Kundalini or the energy of Consciousness (capital "C") informs our human understanding. But there is a paradox here, a dilemma. By the same primordial channel, words like *"self"* and *"other"* inherently corrupt *"how our brain [mind] perceives the environment [world] in which we live."* And if all this were not enough *backstory* to *PartTwo* or how *self/other* mind distorts perception, this adept went on to name the first form of Kundalini:

"...Para-Kundalini is the universal form."

Translating *"Para"* from the Sanskrit, it is a clear reference to a *"supreme"* form, which I intuit, contains the other two forms. And, if I am not mistaken, has been called *"SatCitAnanada"* or *Being-Consciousness-Bliss—"considered a description for the subjective experience of the ultimate unchanging reality."*

—Satcitananda, wikipedia,

Also consider the modern Buddhist point of view: *"Consciousness lies at the very foundation of the known universe, and is mutually independent with the* **information** *it perceives and the phenomena of which it is informed. Each of these three elements is devoid of existence in and of itself, for all three arise in mutual independence."* —Buddhist Scholar B. Alan Wallace

We all might agree that the phenomenon being called Kundalini cannot yet be verified by examination of the human physiology. A similar case of unverifiability could have been said of *psychedelic* phenomena a mere decade ago, before neuroimaging techniques had developed enough to be able to trace the pathways of psychoactive substances in the brain with such precision that we now call it "psychedelic science." I am equally confident that neurophenomenology has a role to play in Kundalini research, but only if these scientists expand their specialties and get their head out of the **brain** scanners and scan the **spinal cord** tissue network.

A future clue to whether neuroscience has changed its priorities will be when we begin to see wholistic depictions of the neurostructures, where the brain is not decapitated at the brain stem, or spinal cord with its own grey matter, is studied with as much enthusiasm as similar tissue in the brain.

In this case, the problem is a medical *bias* in favor of *specialization* rather than a wholistic practice —a *bias* that not only delayed connecting the science of psychedelics to a science of consciousness, but also has stalled the healing and human enlightenment that all the sciences and philosophies, working together, could provide.

The acknowledgement that needs to be made here, and again made in *PartTwo*, is that *BIAS*, be it our own "*self*" interest, professional interest, political interest, financial interest, family interest, any interest, all these, come at the cost of ignoring *the other(s)* on the planet who directly or indirectly will suffer from that conscious or unconscious bias, as will civilization itself.

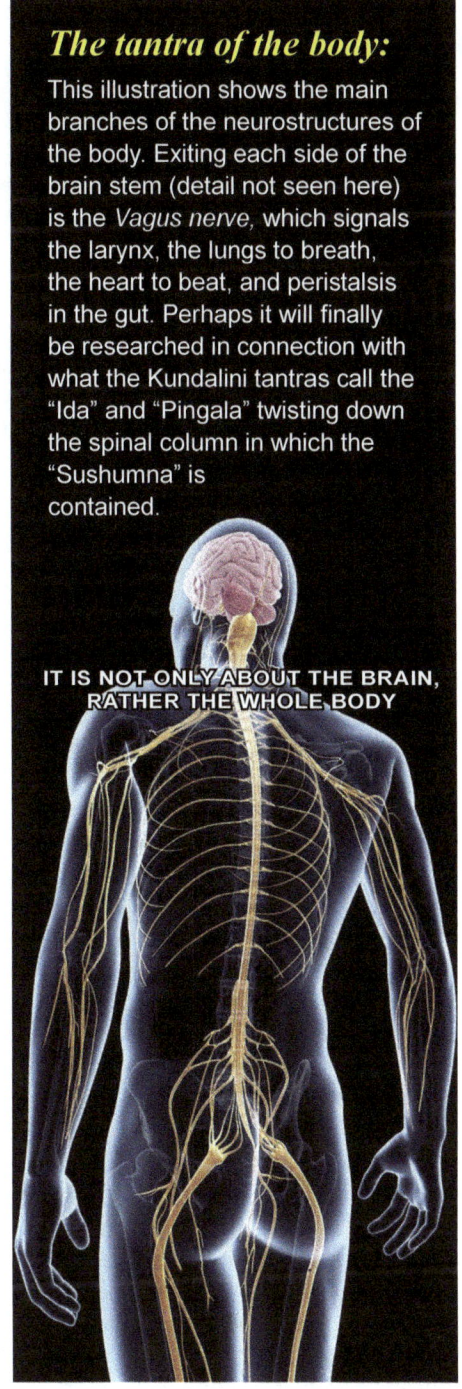

The tantra of the body:

This illustration shows the main branches of the neurostructures of the body. Exiting each side of the brain stem (detail not seen here) is the *Vagus nerve,* which signals the larynx, the lungs to breath, the heart to beat, and peristalsis in the gut. Perhaps it will finally be researched in connection with what the Kundalini tantras call the "Ida" and "Pingala" twisting down the spinal column in which the "Sushumna" is contained.

IT IS NOT ONLY ABOUT THE BRAIN, RATHER THE WHOLE BODY

Not directly related to the topic of kundalini, but certainly related to the psychedelic 60's and how I began *PartOne*, there is the story of what people did, or might do, even today, to explore the *message* they received in the psychedelic experience, whether kundalini is part of that or not.

Perhaps one of the better known examples (at the time) of how one might follow up on their "reality shattering" experience, is that of Richard Alpert, aka Ram Dass. Like him, you might seek out the reality-teachings of ancient Hinduism and take off for India.

But as a Westerner, like Richard, you would likely experience culture shock. And as he tells it, after all kinds of adverse travel mishaps, coming upon his destined teacher and seeing his travel guide prostrate at the feet of his teacher Maharajji Neem Karoli Baba, in the traditional manner of a devotee, Richard thought to himself: **"Oh no! I'm not kissing this guy's feet."** Yet, only a few days later, he was surrendered in a moment not unlike my own surrender event, where I knew instantly that I was in the *presence* of my teacher, my guru, Kundalini—love-bliss itself. Ram Dass had found his message and would bring it back to those of like mind, who wanted to begin the *"work."*

If my reader is familiar with Ram Dass, you likely know of his 1971 book titled *Remember Be Here Now*— the first important book to be received by the psychedelic culture, and by the alternative culture at large. Perhaps, since the *message* and the *work* were for a "New Age," the message was destined to be framed in an entirely new manner, which I came to call *"metagraphics,"* beyond *paragraphics* or ordinary grammar.

The book was unique in its typographic production. The words of the text were put on the page[1] like orchestrated gestures—each person in the production group was assigned a rubber stamp of a letter, a word, or a punctuation mark, and in proper turn, hand-stamped the page. Letters of various sizes created tone, and emphasis.

Actually, there were two books of this extraordinary sort. The second book used more or less conventional typography providing a formal orchestration, rather than the casual harmony evidenced in *Be here Now*. This other book is by the Sufi, Pir Vilayat Inayat Khan, and titled *Toward the One the Perfection Of Love Harmony and Beauty The Only Being*. *See panel p.42*

The two books were published three years apart and became for me and many others a companion set. The Sufi book was purposely designed to achieve that companion look, which should be no surprise considering both authors had a connection to the same eclectic spiritual community called Lama Foundation. The matching size *square*-cut folio was quite intentional— a mandala indicating the *four cornered* world or supposed solid material realm, through which the *light* must pass before it can be feelingly-observed by mind or self.

These strange square books, which themselves came out of the power of community, evidently had the power to create and sustain **virtual community** and certainly before anyone would hear of something called *social media*. Enlightening forces were not only acting on the authors but on the readers—waking up to revolutionary notions of oneness if not the evolutionary flaw inherent in *egohood*.

---

[1]Twice the size of the published version. After publication the oversize pages were sealed up in the adobe walls of some of the buldings at Lama Foundation located near Questa, New Mexico, USA.

The "New Age" was a desire for the oneness and solidarity of **community** —its seeking, its creation, and its inevitable struggle. My own seeking is exemplified in my story of Castalia at Millbrook and my broken-hearted approach to that community. However, after I read *Remember: Be Here Now* ten years later, I did enjoy a retreat stay at Lama Foundation, And those oversize pages I mentioned in the footnote on the preceeding page, I was shown some of them stuffed into a hole in the adobe walls of one of the main buildings

I recall keeping up with the news of the New Age communities birthed in the 60's and 70's, and their rapid decline in the '80s, and disappearance in the '90's, except for the community that produced *Remember: Be Here Now*—so too, the book is still in print, these 50 years later.

Alternative and intentional community is an anomaly today. Generally, most of the hundreds of ad hoc communities that formed in those decades were indeed the refugee encampments for people finding the mainstream either unsafe or intolerant of their brave new consciousness and looking for the **good company** of those whose vision was simpler, neither righteous, grandiose, nor even practical, in most cases.

But, like you perhaps, I let the decades slip by without making any real commitment to community—satisfied with the feeling of oneness vicariously enjoyed in the pages of these books.

People, the world over, who did commit to community, found common ground and nurtured it until it was simply time to move on. Many of the encampments that disbanded or dissolved, did so not out of futility, but rather out of fulfillment.

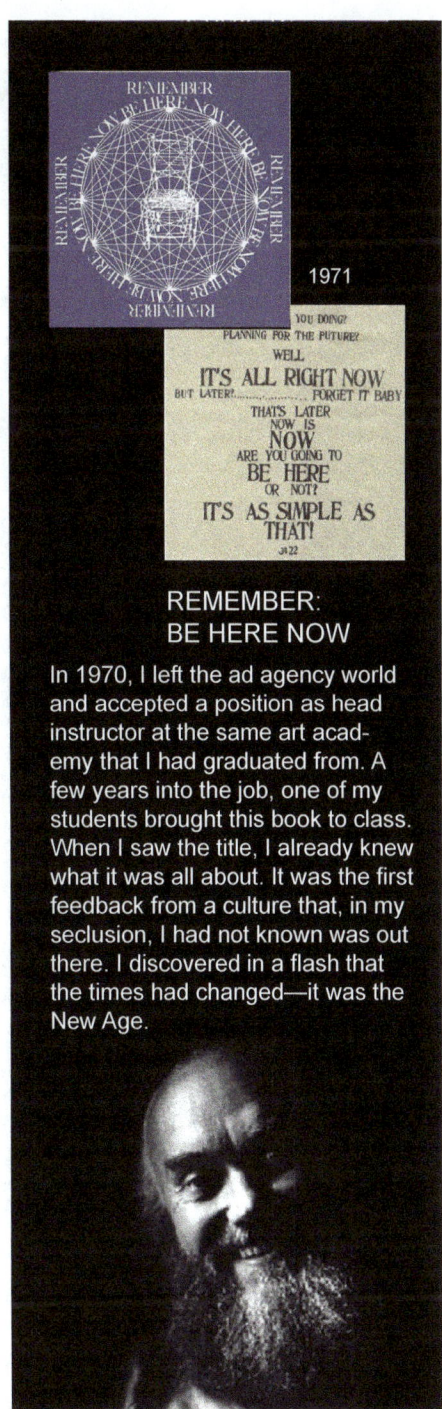

1971

REMEMBER:
BE HERE NOW

In 1970, I left the ad agency world and accepted a position as head instructor at the same art academy that I had graduated from. A few years into the job, one of my students brought this book to class. When I saw the title, I already knew what it was all about. It was the first feedback from a culture that, in my seclusion, I had not known was out there. I discovered in a flash that the times had changed—it was the New Age.

Ram Dass, aka, R.Alpert, PhD., 1931- 2019

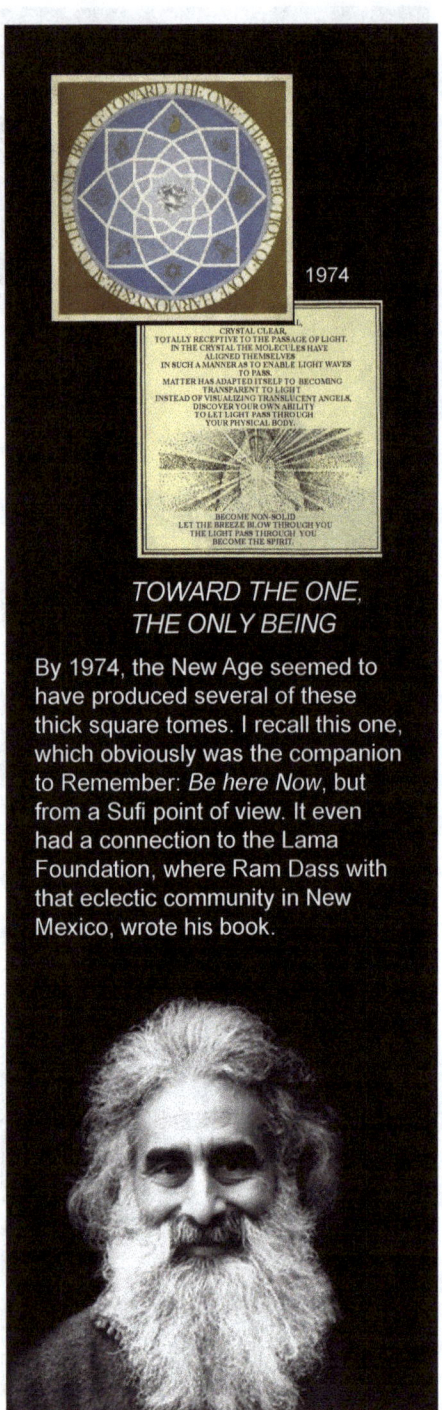

1974

CRYSTAL CLEAR,
TOTALLY RECEPTIVE TO THE PASSAGE OF LIGHT.
IN THE CRYSTAL THE MOLECULES HAVE
ALIGNED THEMSELVES
IN SUCH A MANNER AS TO ENABLE LIGHT WAVES
TO PASS.
MATTER HAS ADAPTED ITSELF TO BECOMING
TRANSPARENT TO LIGHT
INSTEAD OF VISUALIZING TRANSLUCENT ANGELS,
DISCOVER YOUR OWN ABILITY
TO LET LIGHT PASS THROUGH
YOUR PHYSICAL BODY.

BECOME NON-SOLID
LET THE BREEZE BLOW THROUGH YOU
THE LIGHT PASS THROUGH YOU
BECOME THE SPIRIT.

TOWARD THE ONE, THE ONLY BEING

By 1974, the New Age seemed to have produced several of these thick square tomes. I recall this one, which obviously was the companion to Remember: *Be here Now*, but from a Sufi point of view. It even had a connection to the Lama Foundation, where Ram Dass with that eclectic community in New Mexico, wrote his book.

Pir Vilayat Inayat Khan, Sufi Order, 1916-2004

The results are evident in present-day, so-called *"integral"* institutions, universities, and enterprises. The cultural paradigm shifts back then are now the established tributary waters feeding the mainstream. And perhaps it is still the **desire for the oneness** derived from community, more than its ultimate sustainability that will always be behind the **great experiment** that truly defines co-operative community.

Certainly, other evolutionary forces were in transition during that *renaissance* we called the *New Age*. For a while the psychedelic culture and the repurposed wisdom traditions, seemed to indeed be **thriving**. But in only a few decades these forces faded, mainly from delusions of enlightenment and a slipping back into otherwise unaffected, uncaring scientism and consumerism.

Even today, there are two different psychedelic cultural hopes: *Entheogenic Awakening* or Godhood popularized as *"The Psychedelic Renaissance,"* and on the other hand *"Psychedelic Science,"* which seeks remedy for the trauma inherent in *Egohood,* such as PTSD and addiction. As one who was there in the Nixonian political climate, I would caution the public relation departments of either, or both camps, to avoid using words like *"cure, awaken, ecstasy, gurus or Godhood,"* for fear that all your work will again be derailed. The adage: *"History tends to repeat itself"* may apply.

And certainly 50 years, or so, is not much history, but consider even the more ancient history of psychedelics and why psychoactive substances have been kept secret from the general culture, and how their influence on the mystery or esoteric faction of exoteric religions and spiritual traditions survive.

By 1975, a decade after my LSD session, I had arrived at the confluence of four streams of the *message:* Ram Dass and the yogi message *"Remember: Be Here Now,"* Pir Vilayat and the Sufi message *"Toward The One, the Only Being,"* Trungpa and the Buddhist message *"Cutting Through Spiritual Materialism,"* Tim Leary and the revolutionary message *"Drop Out."*

However, I felt no impulse to pursue any of these as the *"work."* But, so as not to lose the memory of this confluence, I made detailed notes about all this, and went on with my advertising art career. Then near the end of the 1970's, I took a break in my ad man career, to teach graphic art and design. And during summers off, I wrote *Metasphere: The Altered State of Word,* published in 1980. Although the subtitle was clearly code for the psychedelic experience, for fear of harming my professional career, I left my own experience out of the book, using instead the cover of ecstatic quotes from ancient mystics and philosophers in the style of an anthology. The rest of the book began an illustrated narrative about "sacred geometries" from which I would later posit a *septenary geometry of mind* that I named *"metaspheric perspective."*

By then I had left teaching, and with no more summers off, it was not until I retired from corporate advertising that I had the time to write *What Always Comes to Mind,* published in 2016. But later, a supportive reviewer explained: *"If it is metaspheric perspective that always comes to mind, then you '***buried the lead***,' a common mistake by new writers."* He suggested I rewrite the book, in three parts: experience first, research second, and practice third.

This *PartOne* has been *metaspheric perspective* as a mystic might experience it. *PartTwo* is how a phenomenologist might describe it with supporting research—a model of mind heretofore unnoticed—information stating the evidence and the issue or problem with it, and a means toward solving that issue. In the academic world such a paper is called a *"White Paper."* However, when sourced outside of academia, it is called a *"Grey Paper,"* especially when the contributing expositors, like myself, are seen as *"outliers."*

Phenomenology is formally defined as the study of structures of consciousness (i.e. mind) from the **first-person perspective**. And yes, *PartOne* was indeed told in the first-person, but I am now talking about "a study" of such a process. To do this I invite you to a symposium or virtual round table *(next page)* of discoverers whose discoveries support *metaspheric perspective.*

PartThree applies *metaspheric perspective (mind)* to a *"game model"* for remedial practice, which argues against the prevailing view that science can solve the climate crisis, ignoring both the conscious and unconscious part *everyone plays* in its cause. Merely by having presumed a separate self *(metaspheric perspective)* we each have unavoidably entered into an *evolutionary* contract of **self-first** interest in preserving *"self"* at the expense of *other (selfs)* on the planet. That *self-first* reflex served us when predators more dominant than humans existed. But in this post-industrial age, the predator species is our own. And since we cannot expect that evolutionary momentum to turn on a dime, its necessary for everyone to consider *repurposing* that *self-first* directive. ▲

THIS CIRCLE OF OUTLIERS SUPPORT THE LOGIC OF A METASPHERIC MODEL OF MIND.

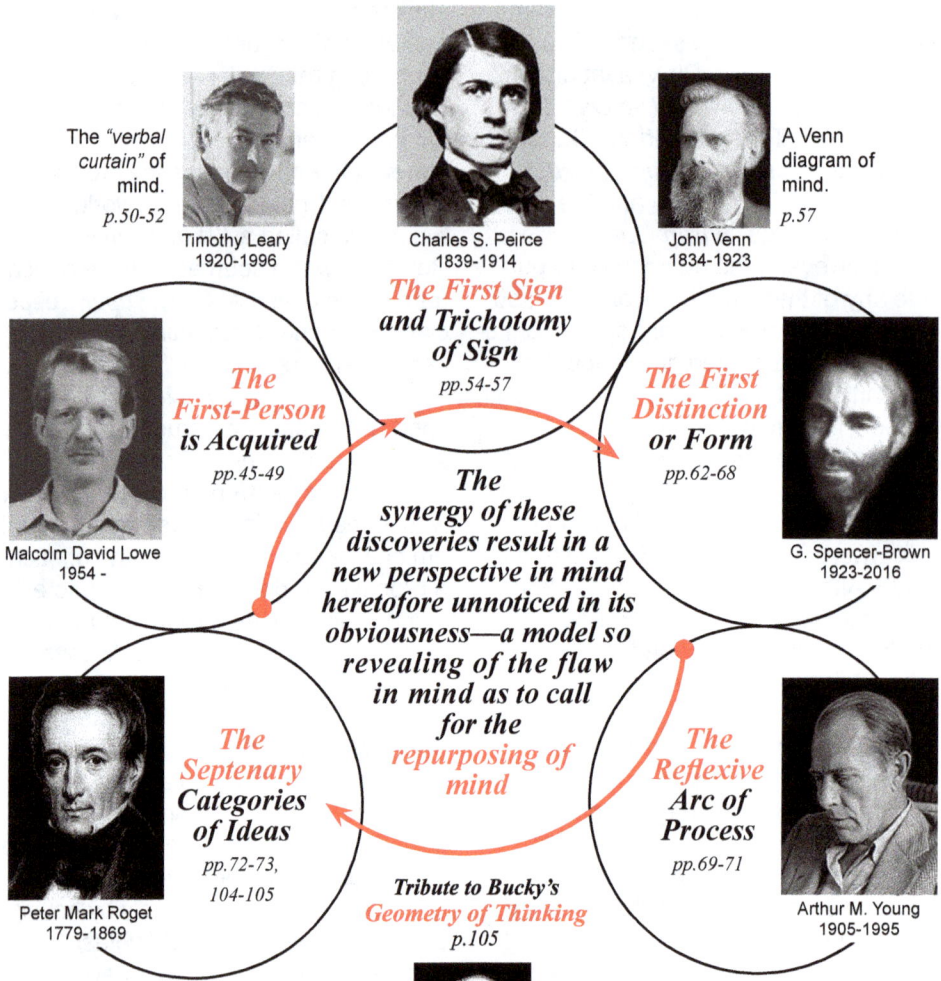

One might assume that all discoveries about mind would, or should, come from psychologists. But, with the exception of the psychologist Timothy Leary and his two cohorts, this has not always proved to be true. Rather, the more extraordinarily useful discoveries seem to come from phenomenologists. Although only one or two of these outliers are formally identified as phenomenologists, all of them had the simplist of intuitions about the most elemental laws of the phenomena of mind—laws that, when brought together, form the necessary *perspective* in mind so desperately needed today.

Part Two
Acquiring Mind
THE GREY PAPER
THE PHENOMENOLOGY OF METASPHERIC PERSPECTIVE

In *PartOne* I used two new terms *"metagraphic,"* and *"metaspheric perspective."* Together these ideas (words or signs) give name to the **model of mind** that will be developed by your own heuristic, as well as the theoretical discoveries in this part, *PartTwo* of the book. The *work,* at times, will touch back to the *message* transmitted, if not received, in *PartOne*.

To, again, quote Alan Watts:

"...if you get the message, hang up the phone, ...go away and work on what you have seen." (PartOne, p.1)

Although some *"work"* has already been done in *PartOne*, this *Paper* explores *mind* as the evolutionary construct in which the *"work"* occurs. And I promise that this **metaspheric model of mind** will prove to be no more complicated than the anecdote told in the *Preface[1]*. And once the model is in mind, how to *repurpose mind* will be surprisingly obvious—*Plug and Play.*

However, given the apocalyptic crises at hand and urgency to do the repurposing immediately, the inconvenient truth is that the work in discovering the model will take the whole of *PartTwo* to prove its integrity and workability. Admittedly, that time consuming effort will be fascinating for some and less so for others.

I begin, and without intrepadition, with the question that I feared to ask my friend Tim Leary: *"Is there really only one being?"* And although I have asked that question of myself over the decades, only recently did I hear it asked in public, posed somewhat differently, and perhaps with even more startling impact:

"How do I know that I am not you, my body, the doorjamb or the trees outside my window, or... specific to each of you here, how do you know that you are not the person sitting next to you?" [ML]

Malcolm David Lowe posed that question in a *Paper* that he presented at *Science of Consciousness 2018,* a conference of neuroscientists, quantum physicists, philosophers, and citizen phenomenologists like myself.

"On its face [it] sounds like an absurd question. Of course you know, although almost certainly you don't know how or why you know." [ML]

Yet, in the psychedelic state of mind, the question is not at all absurd, for very often it is *"...a time when you [cannot] **distinguish** between what [is] you and what [is] not you."* [ML, 1]

---

[1] Preface, p.xii.   [2] [My brackets] added to quote from ([ML]) Malcolm David Lowe.

Now my friend Malcolm is not, himself, speaking to the psychedelic state; rather, he is referring to a prior state:

"...a time [of undifferentiated oneness] in utero, and before one's 1st anniversary of birth." — Malcolm D. Lowe [My brackets]

and to the revolutionary notion that what makes the distinctions *"doorjamb, trees and the window—you and not you,"* is the *"**acquisition of language**."*

Word as *mind,* thought as word, *"doorjamb, trees and the window,"* might at first seem a leap too far—I might argue there must have been something operative as mind before word. Think about it! Then, without thinking in words, tell me what that was. The critical reader might think that a *visual mind* preceded *verbal mind,* and try using *signs* or even use a *sign*-language to *tell* me so. Which is not to say that verbal and visual phenomena are mutually exclusive, I might say that they are identical. I am told that considerable brain real estate is devoted to the visual or *image-native* process, which is not to imagine that the brain is mind, but does say that acquiring a *verbal language* system makes use of a *native visual system,* and between the two has evolved a *"Meaning System"*ᴹᴸ for every language on earth, many of which, according to Lowe, share systems. The following *"Meaning Map"*ᴹᴸ is excerpted from Lowe's paper.

*Polarity and meaning in the letter "**N**"*

Arc of the Sun   Lowercase "n"   Uppercase "N"

Arc[h]etype: ONE   "one"   "ONE"

Excerpt from Malcolm Lowe's paper Copyright 2018

The dictionary defines *word* as the smallest element with literal or practical *meaning* that may be thought, uttered, or written in isolation. It is in written word that we see isolated elements called *glyphs & letters—signs* for some under-*standing* or even lost *meaning.* And these glyphs contain isolated elements on down to a level no longer in *conscious* awareness. Follow the levels back up and you arrive at a simply more comprehensive sign in the form of *whole words* that can then be put into the larger complex of a sentence, paragraph, and/or *metagraph.*

The illiterate, as well, can be said to think in *elements* of utterance otherwise called words. They may not have acquired the *code* to read and write, but like you and me they need not spell out words to give meaning to their utterance, regardless of the heuristic mapping they are using.

From a phenomenological view, I can follow curious stages in writing and *speech,* affirming Lowe's *"a move from undifferentiated to differentiated."* And from a linguistic perspective, what you are *image-ing* when you write in words is called *logography,* curiously one of a *triad* of formative stages, which include *syllabography and alphabetography,* all of which curiously occur universally in the same sequence in the architecture of all languages on earth.

Furthering Lowe's *"radical idea,"* I will be sharing much earlier outlier views, which build the case for the **metagraphic** model of mind, a term introduced at the start of this paper—perhaps for the first time, a way for us all to see how

"...the world is constructed in such a way as to see itself." —G. Spencer-Brown

"The General Architecture of Language Holds the Key to Consciousness"

A Paper by Malcolm David Lowe, 2018
Selected short excerpt [with my brackets]:

"My radical idea is that consciousness [mind] is a construct of human language... All languages contain the same design feature that makes consciousness an inevitable outcome of learning them. If this is true... then the consciousness [mind] you take for granted would collapse without languages [of some kind].

The reason I bring up this perceptual divide between things **'ME'** *and things* **'OTHER'** *is that it cuts to the heart of who we are as conscious beings. Each of us knows that we stand apart from all of the things we see out there in the world and all actions or periods of time that have a temporal existence... We are very clear about the boundaries [spheres] between what is ME and What is Not Me.*

My contention is that... Somewhere in here between birth and present you acquired your first language—your mother tongue—a Meaning System was installed...

My claim is that... this caused you to move or transition from **an undifferentiated being to a differentiated, conscious one...**

The installation of a Meaning System caused a **separation** *to occur between you (as you) and the rest of the world. Initially a wedge, later it became a gulf. And the effect... was to tease apart the Subject* **'Me'** *(and later* **'I'***) from all Others, to that point you perceive things today—a world [reality] of conceptual entities that are quite distinct from you...*

Of course this transition was completely seamless and unconscious and remains out of your conscious mind today... It is not the eyes that allow you to see. The eyes see nothing. They are merely receptors that process light...it is **the inner 'I'** *that interprets the information piped in from the senses."* [My brackets & bold]

Note: Malcolm and I met at Science of Consciousness 2018, a conference where we both were presenting papers. It struck me that his "Radical Idea" provides the necessary first, or prior, insight into the metaspheric model of mind. Selected excerpts of his presentation are reprinted with his permission.

A linguist[1] might tell us that the word *"number"* derives from the Proto-Indo-European root *nem-* *"to divide,"* which, if I am not mistaken, is what we have been talking about. And if I understand Lowe's discovery, it is the *"acquisition of language"* that has apparently *divided* the *default state* of consciousness *"from undifferentiated being to a differentiated conscious one."*

Lowe, who insists he is not a linguist, makes his point with the analogue of a *"virtual reality helmet that modifies reality."* So, I have taken his analogue and with my artistic license, show how such a *"helmet"* fits the **"first person"** in the long established *Deixis[2] of Person, Place, and Time*. Looking at the panel, note how Lowe's thesis on *SELF* and *OTHER* so easily introduces *deictic expression*. Also consider that *deixis* is likely the first realization of *number in human awareness*.

Later on in this paper, a *2-page[3] spread* is devoted to a *"virtual headgear"* more revealing of the form of reality than mere three-part deictic grammar—revealing a seven-part or **septenary form** of reality itself. But we have some work ahead to get there, so be patient with your "self." This new perspective might look much like an expanded *deictic*, but I simply call it *metaspheric perspective.*

Even with your current perspective, what comes to mind, before the model comes into full view, is how the **self/other** construct was evolutionarily beneficial, yet now that same duality can be terribly destructive, demonstrated historically in *self-first* tribalism, war, right/left politics, the *wealth/poverty gap*, and certainly in the current *mass extinction* of non-human species and wanton depletion of resources on this planet.

Before moving on, one might ask, is the acquisition of language the whole story of how that *first-person* came to be? And are we talking about "person" as an *organism*, or more about how mind itself, the agency of *differentiation*, came to be? Curiously, an *organism* is defined as a contiguous system of *cells*, and the interesting thing about a *cell* is that around 3.5 billion years ago, contiguous systems of replicating molecules or pre-biotic chemicals, somehow strategically partitioned[4] themselves into a membrane or *cell ("small room")—"a One in a sea of Ones."* ᴹᴸ

Likewise, compare the bits and bytes of the fundamental elements of language to those fundamental *pre-biotic* elements that eventually come together to partition thought into digestible units of sign, word, and sentence—one period (.) of thought at a time. This partitioning seems an unavoidable, if not the **necessary** function of mind, so that *"you"* as *"undifferentiated consciousness "can* actually function as a *"differentiated conscious one... in a sea of Ones,"* ᴹᴸ or other "I"s.

There are also other phenomena, than Lowe's discovery, that otherwise support *undifferentiated [or transcendent] consciousness*. To begin with, there is that disturbingly simple and paradoxical perspective of the artist who obviously is transcendent to the page (49) upon which he drew this diagram of *deictic expression,* as well as the reader, transcendent to the drawing.

Ironically we are after a model of mind that happens to already be in mind, already in play, but to see both its flaw and promise requires we look at it from that undifferentiated or transcendent place, prior to differentiation.

---

[1] Lowe might insist that he is not a linguist, rather a student of consciousness. [2] Deixis, see caption bottom of panel. [3] G. Spencer-Brown's *Laws of Form*, pp.122-123. [4 and 7] See circle photo in panel, bottom right next page.

Acquiring Mind — THE acquisition OF number

LOWE'S "VIRTUAL REALITY HELMET" EXPLAINS THE **FIRST-PERSON** DEIXIS.

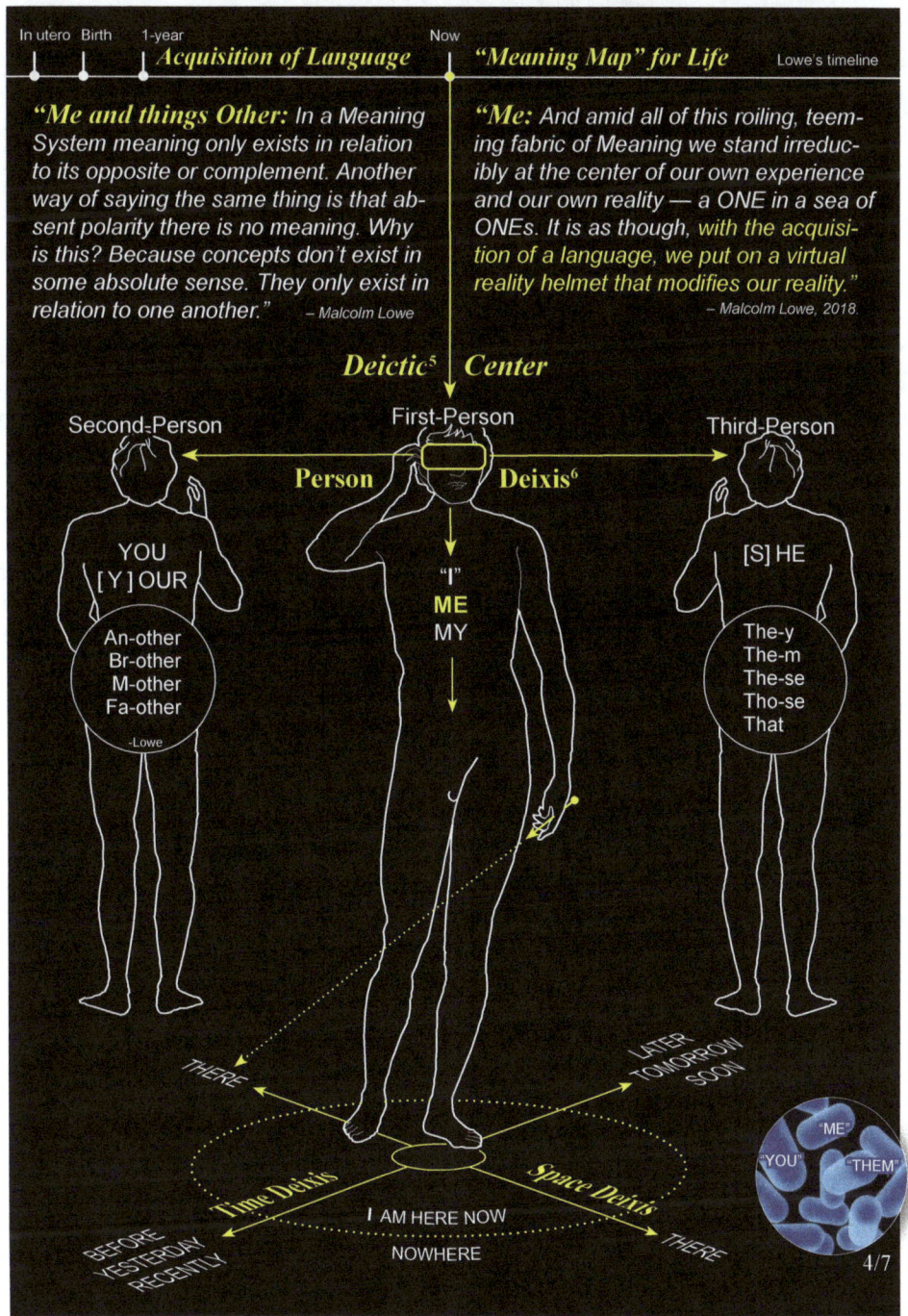

"Me and things Other: In a Meaning System meaning only exists in relation to its opposite or complement. Another way of saying the same thing is that absent polarity there is no meaning. Why is this? Because concepts don't exist in some absolute sense. They only exist in relation to one another." — Malcolm Lowe

"Me: And amid all of this roiling, teeming fabric of Meaning we stand irreducibly at the center of our own experience and our own reality — a ONE in a sea of ONEs. It is as though, *with the acquisition of a language, we put on a virtual reality helmet that modifies our reality."* — Malcolm Lowe, 2018.

[5] "Deictic" is pronounced dactic. [6] "Deixis", Gk "deiknynai" to point, as to other. www.wikipedia.org. Such a diagram is common, but note my addition of Lowe's VR Helmet ▬. [4 and 7] 3.5 billion years ago pre-biotic life separated out (partitoned itsef) from the "other".

Any model of mind needs to be seen from outside real mind or examined as you would an object of art, or tool. It needs to be in the palm of your hand, so to speak—perhaps drawn on a piece of paper. This might have a name: *mindhacking,* and unlike *neurohacking,* we can only do this by *phenomenological* means, or:

"... the study of structures of consciousness experienced from the first-person point of view." —wikipedia.com/phenomenology

"A phenomenological model is characterized as being completely independent of theory while incorporating principles and laws associated with theory."
—The Stanford Encyclopedia of Phenomenology.com

Certainly these outliers were *theorists, logicians, visualists, first person mindhackers*—chipping away at a larger, already extant, model. Separated in place and times[1], perhaps they found each other's work, just as I found theirs; perhaps not. It is no surprise that today in the latest journals of phenomenology, three[2] have been closely linked together as to the mutually connecting fragments in their work. Each having a different piece of mind (the model) —given the *undifferentiated* side of reality against which the model is placed.

Also, perhaps of no surprise to my reader, I included Timothy Leary somewhere in my list of outliers, not merely for his own version of mindhacking, rather for his insight in coining the phrase: *"the verbal curtain"* of mind which further highlights the connection between language, mind, and the merely virtual reality we call duality.

*"He is admitted into the select group of those who have passed through the **verbal curtain** into other modes of consciousness."*
–Tim Leary, Politics of Ecstasy, Also see next page.

A *"select group"* perhaps, but not for the reasons you might suspect, rather because any conscious (thinking) *command* to *self* to *"pass through,"* even with the best yogic discipline or meditative intention, will not permit such passage —for it is only in <u>spontaneously losing self,</u> that one might pass through. That spontaneity may or may not happen even as a result of ingesting an entheogen. The notion that reality is an *"undividable oneness"* is not our ordinarily thinking experience, nor even fathomable by mind, but it is also likely that you are reading this book because of some ordinary *or extra*-ordinary experience which may have allowed you to break through that *"verbal curtain."*

And what better way of explaining this than our quasi-Socratic method applied to the evolution or development of written and spoken word. Such study[3] explains the progression from Lowe's *"helmet of language,"* or *first person* to Leary's *"verbal curtain"* to the separating out from *"scripturia continua,[4]"* to Roget's insistence on the agency of word(s) as the *"instruments of thought,"* —all leading to Spencer-Brown's *first distinction,* via Peirce's *first sign,* and Young's *"reflexive universe."*

All that, is the languaged glue that will hold the final model together—the *metaspheric model* ⋛ —ready for use, ready to be repurposed as a conscious means of correcting the evolutionary flaw of self-first reflexive mind.

---

[1] Graphic p.44. [2] Namely Peirce, Spencer-Brown, and Young. [3] Beginning next page. [4] p.52.

Acquiring Mind THE verbal curtain OF mind

PASSING THROUGH VERBAL MIND TO OTHER MODES OF CONSCIOUSNESS

1888 wood cut by unknown artist for the book *L'atmosphere* by meteorologist Camille Flammarian. (Adapted somewhat by the author for his purposes.).

Leary's *"verbal curtain"* opens both ways, *separating out "from undifferentiated being to a differentiated, conscious one,"* ^{ML} and vice versa. It is the isolating or *separating out* that is both the advantage and disadvantage to life and consciousness—the flaw in *evolved* mind. Mind, as it is now, can be said to be obsolete, or at least the purposeful structure of mind is obsolete. So you might ask, why give me a model of the flawed mind? The answer is that once you inspect the flaw, you might likely move **toward repurposing mind**, and the urgency involved will likewise be glaringly obvious.

The *separating out from undifferentiated being to a differentiated, conscious one"* is difficult to merely ponder, so it will help to back up a little and illustrate what it is that was *undifferentiated* and how and why, over time, it has been separated out *(differentiated)*.

"Early writing goes on without breaks between words or after sentences and paragraphs. When a break in the sense occurred, a mark was made beside that line. This was called a paragraph, para meaning beside. When divisions were made, the term was transferred to the division. A comma, meaning to cut, was a small section of a passage. The longer passage was called a period, meaning course or circuit of thought.[1]"

That *"going on without breaks"* is called "**Scriptura Continua**;"[2] although incomprehensible today, it gives a historical candid view into *"acquisition of language"*^{ML} well after the *"un-dividable oneness"*^{CP} or continuum of *undifferentiated being (or consciousness)* had begun to be divided (separated out).

Inscribed on clay and parchment, it took millennia for further division of the *"undividable"* into *words and phrases*. The *scriptura continua* page was not actually read from, rather used as a crib sheet for a memorized delivery of an oral version of the text. Millennia passed before, in 1495, Aldus Manutius,[3] with his invention of movable type for printing, created modern punctuation—further **separating-out** the underlying oneness of consciousness for the *silent reader* as literacy took hold.

Typical of such revolution in technology, it comes with drawbacks as well as advantages —the disadvantage here is the ever more deepening descent into *duality* from an otherwise intuited default state of *nonduality,* or so the metaphysicians among us might lament.

Scriptura Continua was a late stage of *logography (speech-writing)* that appeared in all languages, mimicking the long established *phonic signs* transmitted in *speech* originally derived from *visual signs*. And when you think about it, *speech*, likewise, *"goes on without breaks."* It is with the listener that breaks are inferred. I can notice this when I listen to an unfamiliar or foreign language. I cannot hear any *breaks* in the transmission of the in-*form*-ation or *"undividable oneness."* If it is our own language, the unbroken transmission is there, but knowing the conventions of the language, my listener **infers** breaks after words and phrases, whereas in the physics of the transmission, there are **no breaks** at all.

If an *actual gap* or pause is perceived by the listener, it can usually be traced to an actual silencing of the transmission, perhaps after a sentence or *"period"* (.) of thought.

---

[1] Excerpt, 15th Edition *Encyclopaedia Britannica*.   [2] Example, previous page.   [3] 1450-1515.

SCRIPTURA CONTINUA IS EVIDENCE OF PRIOR UNDIFFERENTIATED ONENESS.

Columns: Greek script and Latin Cursive. When a break in the sense occurred, a mark was made beside that line and called a paragraph, "para" meaning beside—the paragraph was the first unit of grammar prior to the period (.) or sentence and the comma (,) to "cut into" the sentence.

Just as the discovery of Lowe's *"acquisition of language"* holds the key to the *separating out,* or dichotomy, of the *"self/other"* mind, so too it explains the 3-part separating out in the *"deixis[1] of person, time, and place."* That understanding is actually or literally the *after thought,* so to speak, to the intuition of the preceding or prior *"un-dividable"* "oneness" that *"Scriptura Continua"* exemplifies. What more concrete example of the *"un-dividable oneness,"* than mind having no separation from the oneness of consciousness for many thousands of years, which matched there being no separation between words (signs), one from the other. The question here is not how did the separating out of words from *un-separable* consciousness occur, rather "why?" It seems plain that *separating out* has been the very function of mind since the beginning—but what if *convergence,* not *divergence,* is the function of consciousness? That would have mind at odds with consciousness.

Before leaving such a curious stage in writing as *Scriptura Continua,* we might also compare it to another curious *"un-dividable oneness,"* — music or musical notation. Although putting all those *signs* down on paper is critical for the composer and musical performance, reading the score is not at all necessary for the audience and their listening enjoyment. Even for a great composer like Paul McCartney, it is not necessary—for he admits he cannot read or write music. In any case, the same physics in regard to *transmission* of *speech* apply when listening to the *language of music*. But here, even the actual silences and sustained notes communicate *"oneness"* or wholeness of the intuited composition.

My research into the symmetry of the Kundalini chakra system revealed that *seven* was certainly more than merely a superstitious number; rather it was a septenary (3-1-3) *"meaning system"* ᴹᴸ with a *logic* behind it. In fact, I decided to look into the field of logic itself—an area in which I have no formal instruction. It was there that I found the remarkable works of these logicians and phenomenologists[2], in which, for three of them, **seven** was at the center of their thesis, and for one gentleman, the magic number was **three**. That *"threeness"* proved to be the *linchpin* so vital to understanding the symmetry of *"sevenness"* (3-1-3) —although my first notice was threeness (1-1-1) and how all major religions curiously separate out the singularity of their Godhead into theological or philosophical *trinities or triads* such as those listed here:

Christianity: *The Three Persons: God, Son, Holy Ghost;* Hinduism: *Creator, Preserver, Destroyer;* Buddhism: *Trikaya of the three bodies of Buddha;* Taoism: *The Three Clarities;* Vedanta: *The Three Realities. In Islam,* everything is done in *cycles of three.*

And while researching all that, one cannot ignore the Seven days of creation, Seven heavens, Seven stages of life, and many other septenaries.

In considering *threeness,* I came across **Charles. S. Peirce**[3] and his ***"Trichotomy of Sign,"*** where one must dive into his thousands of pages of writings to see his full genius around the threeness of sign. Actually, I was quite unaware that the pursuit of *trichotomies* is itself considered a philosophy:

---

[1] deixis, p.49. [2] p.44. [3] Peirce is pronounced purse.

Examples of trichotomies:
Hegel: *thesis, antithesis, synthesis;*
Freud: *id, ego, supergo;*
Kant: *universality, plurality, totality;*
Lacan: *real, symbolic, imaginary;*
St. Agustine: *divine, natural, human;*
St. Paul: *body, soul, spirit;*

— From a longer list: wikipedia/trichotomy

The more familiar *"trichotomy"* is the awareness of **time** separated into: *past, future, present.* Likewise, similar to how we observe dimensional **space**, in its threeness present all at once.

As for Peirce's consideration, it is all about sign: the *"sign-itself,"* its *object-sign,"* and thirdly, what he calls its *"interpret<u>ant.</u>"* He begins:

"Signs are divisible by three; first as the sign in itself... a mere quality... [apparent reality]... secondly as the relation of sign to its object... having some... existential relation to that object, or in its relation to an interpretant; thirdly as its Interpretant represents it as a sign of possibility... or a sign of reason [the operation of mind]." - Peirce [My brackets]

"THOUGHT-SIGNS"

"Peirce is keen to associate signs with cognition. In particular, Peirce claims that all thought is in signs (W2. 213). We can see this from Peirce's early idea that every interpretant is itself a further sign of the signified object. Since interpretants are the interpreting thoughts we have of signifying relations, and these interpreting thoughts are themselves signs, it seems to be a straightforward consequence that all thoughts are signs, or as Peirce calls them 'thought-signs.'"

— Stanford Encyclopedia of Philosophy [My brackets]

A true outlier

"Merely to say that Peirce was extremely fond of... triadic relations, would fail miserably to do justice to the overwhelming obtrusiveness in his philosophy of the number three. Indeed, he made the most fundamental categories of all "things" of any sort whatsoever the categories of Firstness, Secondness, and Thirdness, and he often described "things" as being "firsts" or "seconds" or "thirds." - http://plato.stanford.edu/entries/peirce/#access

"I define sign as anything which is so determined by something else, called its Object, and so de<u>termines an effect upon a person, which effect I call its Interpretant,</u> that later is thereby immediately determined by the person."

— Charles Peirce, P2,478) [My underline]

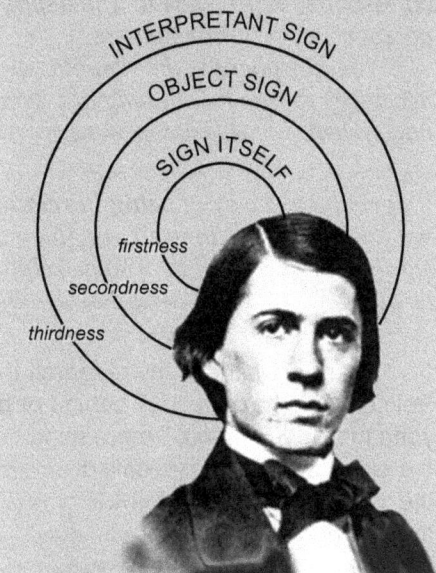

Charles S. Peirce 1839-1914

Perhaps the closest to a plain English understanding of Peircean phenomenology is that reality comes to or is present to mind as *signs (words)* in a 3-part perspective: 1. reality as it appears, 2. as objectified, 3. and as subjectified. That **flow** *of information* defines *"mind,"* and that in-*form*-ation defines *"sign."*

Peirce called his study *of "sign"* **semiosis** (now **semiotics**). I have given only a couple of quotes from his corpus of 100,000 pages, leaving semiotics itself to Peircean scholars to sort out. In other words, although the research is thorough, it is quite briefly stated here—just enough to satisfy the general reader of our, so-called, *Grey Paper.*

Peirce was terribly fond of neologisms, which permeate both his writing and the writings of those who have reworked his work for well over a century. Two words in particular are personally intriguing, in that he too found it necessary to coin them from the Greek: *"phaneroscopy"and "phaneron,"* which correspond respectively to *"metaspheric perspective"* and *"metasphere."*

*"***Semiosphere** *is the semiotic space necessary for the functioning of a semiotic system."* — Lotman 1990. [My boldface.]

*"Signhood is a way of **being in relation**, not a way of being in itself. Anything is a sign — not as itself, but in some relation or other."* – Peirce / Wikipedia. [My boldface.]

There are hints in my research that Peirce would have us look behind or beyond mere *"Signhood,"* mere mind, to the prior consciousness, called:
the *"mystical void"*–Jack Engstrom),
the *"unmarked space"*–G. Spencer-Brown
the *"undividable one-ness,"*–Malcolm D. Lowe

That admonition will be helpful in *PartThree* and is no better echoed in all of Peirce's writings than in the following extraordinarily relevant quote:

"Whereas Firstness means undivided and <u>undividable oneness</u>, Secondness involves the dynamic idea of "<u>otherness</u>," of two-sided consciousness, the experience of action and reaction, stimulus and response, change and resistance to change. (CP:7.538) [My underline]
"Secondness is involved whenever we make an effort, a decision, or discovery; orient ourselves in time and space (CP:5.525,58). *Thirdness embodies continuity, the rule of feeling and action by general principles. ... Thirdness is future-oriented and permits us to predict what is to be, and adapt our attitude accordingly."* - (CP:1.337)

Following up on Peirce's intuition of *"two-sided consciousness,"* and presuming he means **two-sided mind**, it is easy to infer that his *trichotomy of sign* would and does apply to *both sides[1] of mind*. And whereas he assumes some of his own observations are self-evident, with little, if any, need of explanation, I will, at least, attempt an explanation, beginning with a Venn diagram *(panel),* to prove a *fourth* or *interpreter-sign* necessary for Peirce's *trichotomy of sign* to work in the *"semiotic space"* of two-sided mind.

Coming out of the Venn proof is a progression *(Fig 5-8)* that reveals the beginning signs of a *metaspheric model* and its *metagraphic rendering (Fig 8)* ⩘≡. As the *Grey Paper* unfolds, with additional outlier discoveries, the ⩘≡ metagraph's text placeholders will be populated with that discovery.

---

[1] conative and cognitive, pp.58-59.

Acquiring Mind — THE hidden sign

THIS VENN PROOF REVEALS THE HEART OF THE METASPHERIC MODEL OF MIND

In Peirce's semiosis[2]: *"The interpret**ant**-sign is the effect a sign has on a person."*
By *"person,"* we may assume he means the interpret**er**[3] of that "effect,"
who or which, can be interpreted as a "tacit" sign or FOURTHNESS in the semiosis.

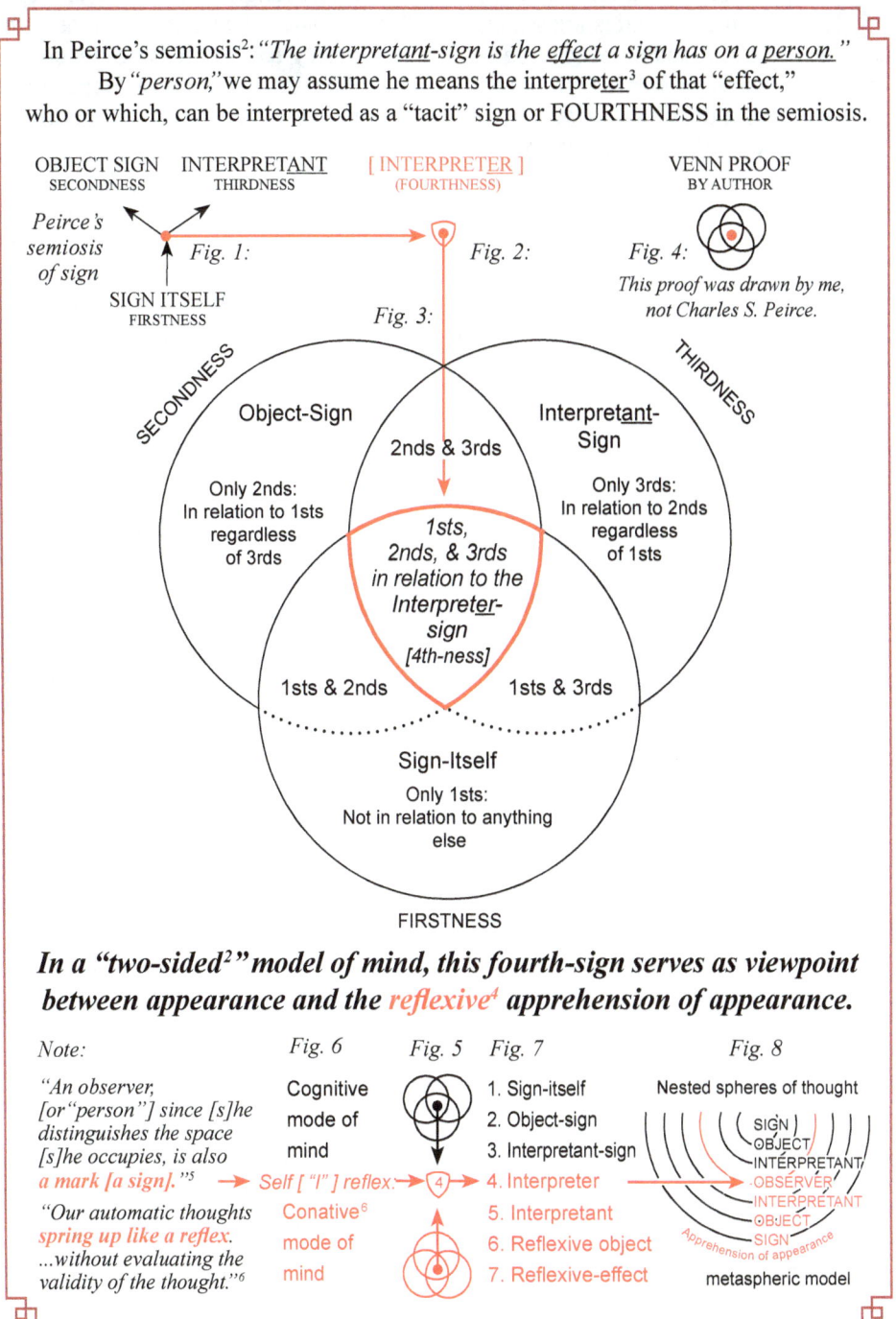

In a "two-sided[2]" model of mind, this fourth-sign serves as viewpoint between appearance and the reflexive[4] apprehension of appearance.

Note:

"An observer, [or "person"] since [s]he distinguishes the space [s]he occupies, is also a mark [a sign]."[5]

"Our automatic thoughts spring up like a reflex. ...without evaluating the validity of the thought."[6]

Fig. 6 — Cognitive mode of mind
Fig. 5 — Self ["I"] reflex:
Conative[6] mode of mind

Fig. 7:
1. Sign-itself
2. Object-sign
3. Interpretant-sign
4. Interpreter
5. Interpretant
6. Reflexive object
7. Reflexive-effect

Fig. 8 — Nested spheres of thought
metaspheric model

---

[2] Process of signification or study of signs. [3] Previous page. [4] Young, pp.69-71. [5] G. Spencer-Brown, 54-60 [My brackets]. [6] Conative vs Cognitive mode of mind, p.58-59 [pp.78-79].

A supportive finding for the reflexive trichotomy of mind is known in, so-called, cognitive science as the *"Modularity of Mind,"* a model of the *"Three modes of intellection":* **cognitive, affectual, and conative.** Yet, somewhere along the way, reference to the **"conative[1]"** mode or *"conation"* fell out of favor with the science very shortly after this *modularity* was proposed, because the Latin root *"conatus,"* or **tendency, impulse, and action** was considered too vague.

However, it is that *"conative"* mode, not the so called *"cognitive"* mode which generates the *reflex bias,* evolutionarily in place, that is always in favor of self, and therefore deserving of examination at least equal to that given the *cognitive* side of mind.

Absent any real understanding of the importance of the *conative module,* present science resorts to putting all the *conative* eggs of *tendency, impulse, and action* into the *cognitive* basket, going so far as to mislabel examples of the *conative* process, in what that science calls the *"Cognitive Bias Codex"* —a title that in so many ways is misleading, and more accurately an excellent example of *scientific bias.*

Using the word *"cognitive"* rather than *"conative"* in naming the *codex* is the first mistake. It suggests a *cognitive disorder* and leaves the impression that *"bias,"* by any of the more than 200 one-line descriptions in the codex, is not *"normal,"* whereas *bias itself* is not only natural, but all *bias (tendency, impulse, and action)* has the same root—*a reflex,* evolutionarily acquired, thus an unavoidable process, having sole *purpose* of protecting, preserving, and providing for, the *"self,"* consciously or otherwise.

Interestingly, most every line of the *Cognitive Bias Codex* begins with **"Tendency to"** —otherwise descriptive of the *conative* mode. Here are a couple of examples from the codex:

#22 "Conservatism: The tendency to revise one's beliefs insufficiently when presented with new evidence. #30 The denomination effect: The tendency to spend money when it is denominated in small amounts like coins rather than in large amounts like bills."

Whereas *cognition* best describes a **passive** or denoting mode, that of *acquiring* information through sensory input, including mind as a sense, overuse of the word *"cognition"* may explain why it has become the psychologist's catchall phrase for *any* kind of thinking whatsoever. However, a recent article breaks with that single minded idea to describe what I am calling the **active** or *"conative reflexive mode"* as something removed from the cognitive mode, calling it *"automatic thought:"*

"Cognitive theory tells us that it is not the situation itself that determines what we feel, but rather it is <u>the way we think</u> about the situation. The thoughts that go through our mind in any given situation are automatic and cause us to have different emotional responses. **Our automatic thoughts spring up like a reflex:** *they are rapid and ofttimes very brief. In fact many people are barely aware of their automatic thoughts and are more likely to notice the emotion that follows. As a result, many people accept their automatic thoughts as being true, without evaluating the validity of the thought."*[2]

---

[1] Conative explained on p.59. [2] Adapted from *Cognitive Therapy*, by Judith H. Beck, [My bold and underline].

THIS METAGRAPH SIMPLIFIES THE VENN CALCULUS FROM THE PRECEDING PANEL.

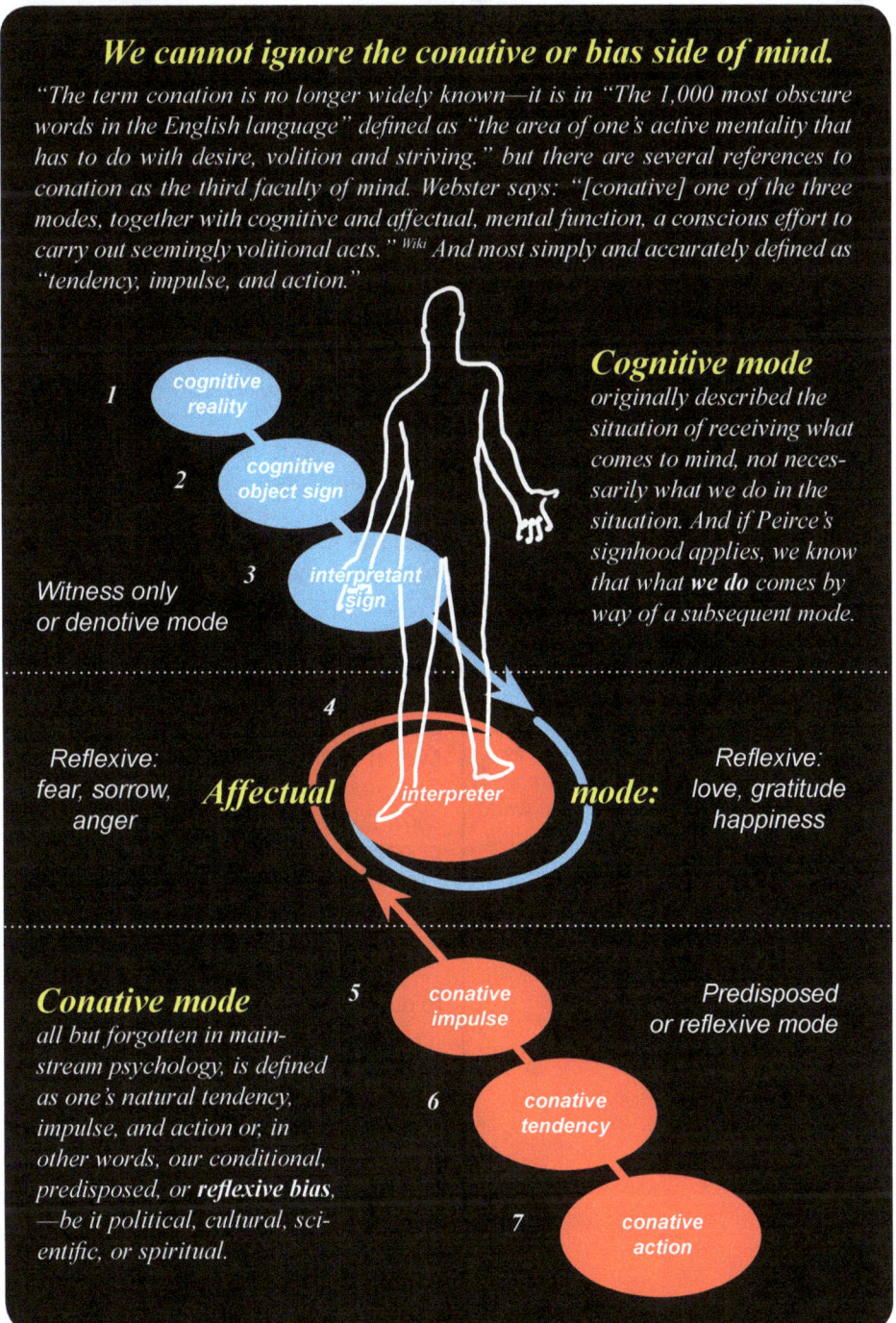

Top third of panel: Peirce's trichotomy applied to the objective side of mind. Bottom third of panel: Peirce's trichotomy applied to the subjective side of mind. [Author's graphic or metagraph.]

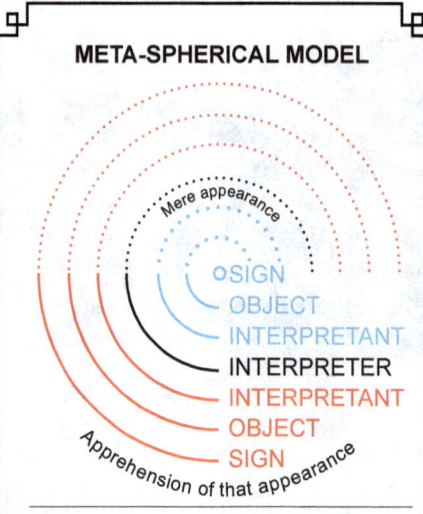

Long after the verbose longhand version of the discoveries made here are forgotten, the metagraph ຝ≡ of the model will serve as an all encompassing shorthand version of the septenary. The point is to attribute a set of laws or rules to *metasphere* (the model or metagraph) that are fixed, or as immutable as any other laws of form. As for the *laws* in this model of mind, the shorthand reads:

ຝ— **Cognitive node:** The mere *appearance* side of mind, witnessing, passive, or the *sign itself* of mind.

ຝ– **Affectual node:** The feeling point of view of "I," *object sign* of mind.

ຝ_ **Conative node:** The active, reflexive, *apprehension* side of mind, evolutionarily biased self-interest, understood as the triad of *tendency, impulse, action* and the dominant side of the thought process, and what Peirce would identify as the *interpretant sign.*

This paper focuses on a step-by-step codifying of the laws most obviously supporting a *metaspheric perspective* on reality, so that the integrity of the final model ຝ≡ is sufficiently formed to allow its use in a thought experiment[1] or personal application that can affect a *repurposing of mind,* sufficient to flatten the present downward curve of civilization due to "self-first" flaw in mind.

I admit that what I am asking you to do in acquiring this model is to use *mind* to make the model, which is like asking the architect to let the building do the work, or something like pulling yourself up by your own boot straps.

If you are unclear what I mean by *first-person* point of view, and impatient with my showing these structures of mind, and collapsing others, pause and appreciate that *ungrounded* feeling, for it is indeed a first-person experience.

---

[1] PartThree p.81-93.

That ungrounded feeling is exactly the mood needed to allow the model to come alive. *Ungrounded* is a difficult place, but think of it like awaiting the *"booting"* process in a computer. They say the effort to go from being a collection of memory chips to a functioning computer is pretty impressive—there is likely some magic involved.

My only advantage is that I already arrived at a *fully booted model* via my entheogenic experience. What we are doing here is backtracking my own pondering and re-search, after-the-fact and over many years, to confirm to you the intuition and integrity of the model.

Further into the booting process, the magic will happen, it will become self-evident that you too, unwittingly, have the same model in mind and are working it as we speak.

What we do not want to do here is to *invent* anything. The model is no more an invention than the so-called **"standard model"** [2] of particle physics. Although language is certainly an artifact, the first criterion for the accuracy or integrity of our model is that it is not man-made. Regardless of how contrived both the model and mind might seem, what we are doing here, is *discovering* a process, its symmetry and number. Its faults and superficiality will become clear, once the model is put on as easily as a hat and experienced through our *first-person "I"s*.

Rather than considering what is drawn on the page to be the thing itself, disciplines like physics, mathematics and phenomenology rather call it a *model* of the thing. This allows one to virtually walk all around the thing, and, if it is transparent enough, then be able to look inside.

Booting up

Reflexive view

of What Is

Seriously, there is indeed some magic, or perhaps just good old fashioned phenomenological steampunk involved, like the *evolutionarily obsolete virtual headgear* that we all unavoidably wear, *which* from the vantage point of the "I" forces us to see reality thrice removed from *what it is*, and again thrice removed from *what we think it is* —a vantage point and obscuration that is tolerable only because we are ordinarily unaware that mind is fashioned in this way. But there is a way to become aware and, with understanding and practice, repurpose mind. To get to that place, we already have the headgear, and to complete the ensemble, special footwear may also help. Put these on and simply follow the directions:

Grab straps and pull yourself up.

[2] p.75.

Unlike Peirce, whose work is a canon of 100,000 pages, the next outlier in this story, this *paper,* is **G. Spencer-Brown** who manages to condense his work into a relatively small book of 140 pages titled *Laws of Form,* first published in London, then in America in 1969. An early reviewer of *LoF* called its thesis "*... the implicit root of cognition: the ability to distinguish.*" My own view is to call it the *explicit* process of mind. Both aspects of *"the cutting up"* or *"distinction-making"* that Spencer-Brown is talking about are exemplified where he says:

"We cannot escape the fact that the world [reality] we know is constructed in order (and thus in such a way as to be able) to see itself. This is indeed amazing. Not so much in view of what it sees, but in respect of the fact that it sees at all. But in order to do so, evidently it must first cut itself up into a least one state which sees, and at least one other state which is seen."[1]

The profound yet simple intuition of G. Spencer-Brown's work is best introduced by a friend of mine, **Randy Dible**[2], in one of his recent papers. Without getting into the symbolic logic *(top of panel)* behind *Laws of Form,* Randy has this insight *(panel next page)* to LoF.

Randy Dible is a professor, speaker, and writer of numerous articles on philosophy of phenomenology.

"*... we have reached a place so primitive that active and passive... have long since condensed together, and any form of words will suggest more categories than [the seven] there really are.*"[3]

G. Spencer-Brown

Logicians know his work primarily for its symbolic calculus in the form of a mark: ⌐ and no mark; equivalents as in ⌐⌐ = ⌐ and steps as in ⌐⌐ → ⌐ and crossings as in ⌐⌐ and cancellations, as in ⌐⌐ →⌐, and so on.

However, we need only skip to the notes in the back of his book, to read the list of the categories of distinction (form) in seven lines of plain English, with my own artful touch of *metaspheric perspective* ⌇≡ *(shown below)*:

"*Laws of Form*"

1. – let a distinction be drawn
2. – let there be a distinction
3. – find a distinction
4. – *See a distinction*
5. – describe a distinction
6. – define a distinction
7. – draw a distinction

G. Spencer-Brown 1923-2016

---

[1] *Laws of Form* (LoF), 1972 edition p.84, [My brackets]. [2] Dible is pronounced like Bible.
[3] LoF, 1972 edition p.84 [My brackets and yellow highlighting].

The "intuitive simplicity" of G. Spencer-Brown's discovery

"First Philosophy and First Distinction"
Ontology and Phenomenology of *Laws of Form*
by Randy Dible

"George Spencer-Brown's Laws of Form is a mathematical treatise that calls for philosophical interpretation. Its core component, the calculus of indications, progresses from the simple act of drawing a distinction, through a number of levels of the indication of that distinction, until it finally reaches the level of real existence and the universe as we know it. While applicable to any special case of indication and semantic expression, this calculus is simultaneously a direct analysis of the underlying and ubiquitous substratum of creation from nothing. This means that *Laws of Form* should be understood as offering a theory of being (an ontology) and a theory of form (a phenomenology) on the common ground of an intuitive simplicity. The calculus of indications gives us a way of understanding *everything*—every possible object, every overall gestalt, every possible world, every 'thing' in both the precise literal sense and the diffuse metaphorical sense—as a form of indication, and all *indication* — the very 'form' codified by this calculus — as based on an original and primary distinction at the boundary between everything and nothing. This ultimate boundary, called '*the first distinction*,' stands in a very peculiar relation to every familiar thing in our conscious experience. *This singular peculiarity* of the first distinction should be regarded on the basis of mathematical ontology, in terms of what is called prima philosophia, first philosophy, and in such terms we can determine its ontological and phenomenological status. First philosophy technically begins with Aristotle ...since being itself can only be studied by being distinguished from the being of things other than itself, and in the first place from that which is beyond being. Spencer-Brown's initial positing of the 'first distinction' from nothing with a simple pragmatic injunction 'Draw a distinction' demands the integration of a first ...cause (sophisticated in its ultra-simplicity) with a ...proximate cause (empirical and naive in its simplicity)..." - Page 1 of 12 [My bold font]

Randolph Dible, "First Philosophy and First Distinction: Ontology and Phenomenology of *Laws of Form*," in *Laws of Form*, " a *Fiftieth Anniversary*, ed. L. H. Kauffman, F. Cummins, R. Dible, L. Conrade, G. Ellsbury, A. Crompton & F. Grote (515-537), pp.515-517.

Randolph Dible is a lecturer in philosophy at St. Joseph's University, NY. His dissertation is titled Universal Ontology of the Infinite Sphere. See list of his publications at https://randolphdible.com.

With *"Laws of Form,"* the septenary or sevenness of the model appears all at once, without the interim help of Venn diagramming to mirror the Peircean trichotomy. Exactly how that happens will be illustrated in the panel spread coming up on *pages 66-67*, which envision the model in what I have been calling *metaspheric perspective,* and, from now on, will refer to as *"metasphere."*

This is as real a perspective as what the visual artist technically calls *linear perspective*. In fact the artist's perspective is a perfect analogue to *metaspheric perspective,* since both work from a **point-of-view**, except visual perspective has to do with what is apparent to the **eye**, and *metasphere* has to do with what is apparent to the **"I."**

By whatever heuristic means, it will help to develop a kind of **headgear** in order to navigate the model, similar to Lowe's *VR helmet*[1], or what I call *"I"ware*. Although imagined about the eyes and head, such virtual headgear has nothing to do with the brain, rather with that aspect of consciousness modified as mind. The *metaspheric* or *"I"ware headgear*[2] is analogous to any linear perspective headgear (see top panel).

The "eye" to *"I"ware* perspective is not directly translatable, there is some loss. However the gist is that, from the **point-of-view** of the "I" ■, what comes to mind is thrice removed from *What Is*, and again thrice removed *(reflexively)* from *what we think* it is. Here is where we need that "booting process" to make the jump in awareness required.

The directive *"put in perspective"* is most often a mere idiom for *"opinioned view,"* with the user having no real intention of actually applying the *laws of perspective* to which the directive refers.

Those laws were discovered a mere 500 years ago, and involve *spatial objects* rendered from the point-of-view of the eye, with such axioms as *horizon, vanishing points, and diminution.* From the beginning and certainly from here on out, it is the intention of this paper to render **mental objects** (signs and words that come to mind) in an equally *lawful* manner as the laws of linear perspective are applied to **spatial objects**.

Spencer-Brown's *Laws of Form* can more directly be called **Laws of Distinction**, especially the *"first distinction,"* as highlighted in Dible's paper:

"This singular peculiarity of the first distinction..." [3]

"Peculiarity" is certainly the right adjective when you think about spacial objects. Which is to say: *peculiarly,* the first distinction or 1st spacial dimension can neither be seen nor **drawn** separate from the 2nd and 3rd dimensions or distinctions, which all come to mind at the same time. Similarly, there is *"peculiarity"* around any first distinction drawn about time and temporal objects, i.e the **obscuration** around *future* and *past,* leaving the distinction called *present* as the peculiar *"now"* which, like space, is the synergy of all three distinctions at once. Actually, such *obscuration* around 1st and 2nd distinctions of the most basic of ideas as space and time, is, according to the Peircean Trichotomy of Sign, applicable to any and **all** 1st and 2nd signs or distinctions that come to mind. Although "space" is the sign or mental object used in the example on *Pg 66-67,* any other sign, idea, word, or mental object can be substituted.

---

[1] pp.48-49.   [2] Facing page, fig 2.   [3] Randolph Dible and LoF, p.63.

Acquiring Mind | THE virtual headgear

"Eye" to "I" Analogue:

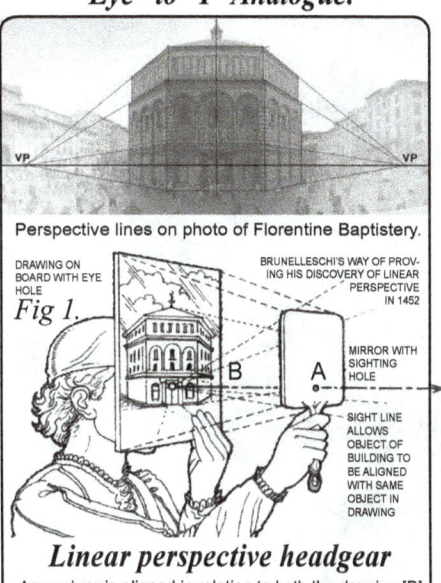

Perspective lines on photo of Florentine Baptistery.

Fig 1.

Linear perspective headgear

As a mirror is aligned in relation to both the drawing [B] and the building [A], and rotated in and out of view, the observer sees the facsimile between the actual building and the reflected (reflexive view) of the drawing.

Metaspheric perspective headgear

Visualize mind as "I"wear with three pairs of lenses or goggles in front and in back of the "I" [4]

Passive
not yet reflexive
cognitive
mind:

Active,
reflexive
conative
mind:

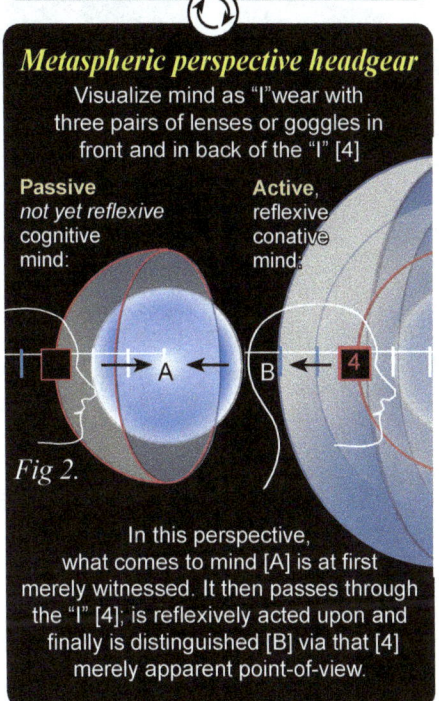

Fig 2.

In this perspective, what comes to mind [A] is at first merely witnessed. It then passes through the "I" [4]; is reflexively acted upon and finally is distinguished [B] via that [4] merely apparent point-of-view.

Summarily illustrated on the *next two pages* is the anticipated synergy or synthesis of Peirce's *"Trichotomy of Sign[4],"* Spencer-Brown's *"Laws of Form [5]"* and Arthur Young's *"Arc ∨ of Process,[6]"* perspectives "*...underlying and ubiquitous substratum of creation [of mind] from nothing.*" R.D., [My bracket].

Up to this point in the book we have used the flat plane or surface of the page to convey (map) the dimensions of *metasphere* (mind). From here on allow your self to transcend the page. Lift what you have discovered up with you into the territory called mind. Put on the special footwear and headgear provided for that *booting* process. Yes, it does seem that mind is in the head, so you will need the *I-ware*. Yet, who knows where mind really resides? Put your "self" at placeholder [4], according to Spencer-Brown's *"See a distinction.[7]"* Be open to the sphericity and concentricity of this space—this *metasphere,* or as the scholarly phenomenologists might call it, this *"Semiosphere[8]."*

Once there, simply enjoy this far land, tour its byways and signs before resorting to the (map) legend on *page 68* for any more reasonable explanation of what this centerpiece reveals to the "I" and to "You," transcendent to the "I," observing it.

As noted above, there is included in the illustration, the discovery of a more modern student of consciousness than Peirce. He is **Arthur M. Young**, whose discovery of *"The Arc of Process,"* like Lowe's contribution,[9] provides another linchpin in the synergy of these discoveries that complete the model. The ∨ in the perspective or path of distinctions, depicts Young's idea of an *"Arc"* to any process — especially in the reflexive process called mind and likewise in every other category of ideas.

---

[4]Peirce, p.55. [5]Spencer-Brown p.62. [6]Young, p.68. [7]p.67, distinction#4. [8]p.48. [9]Lowe, acquisition of language [or acquisition of mind], p.47.

COGNITIVE OR PASSIVE DISTINCTIONS ARE THE FIRST TO COME TO MIND,

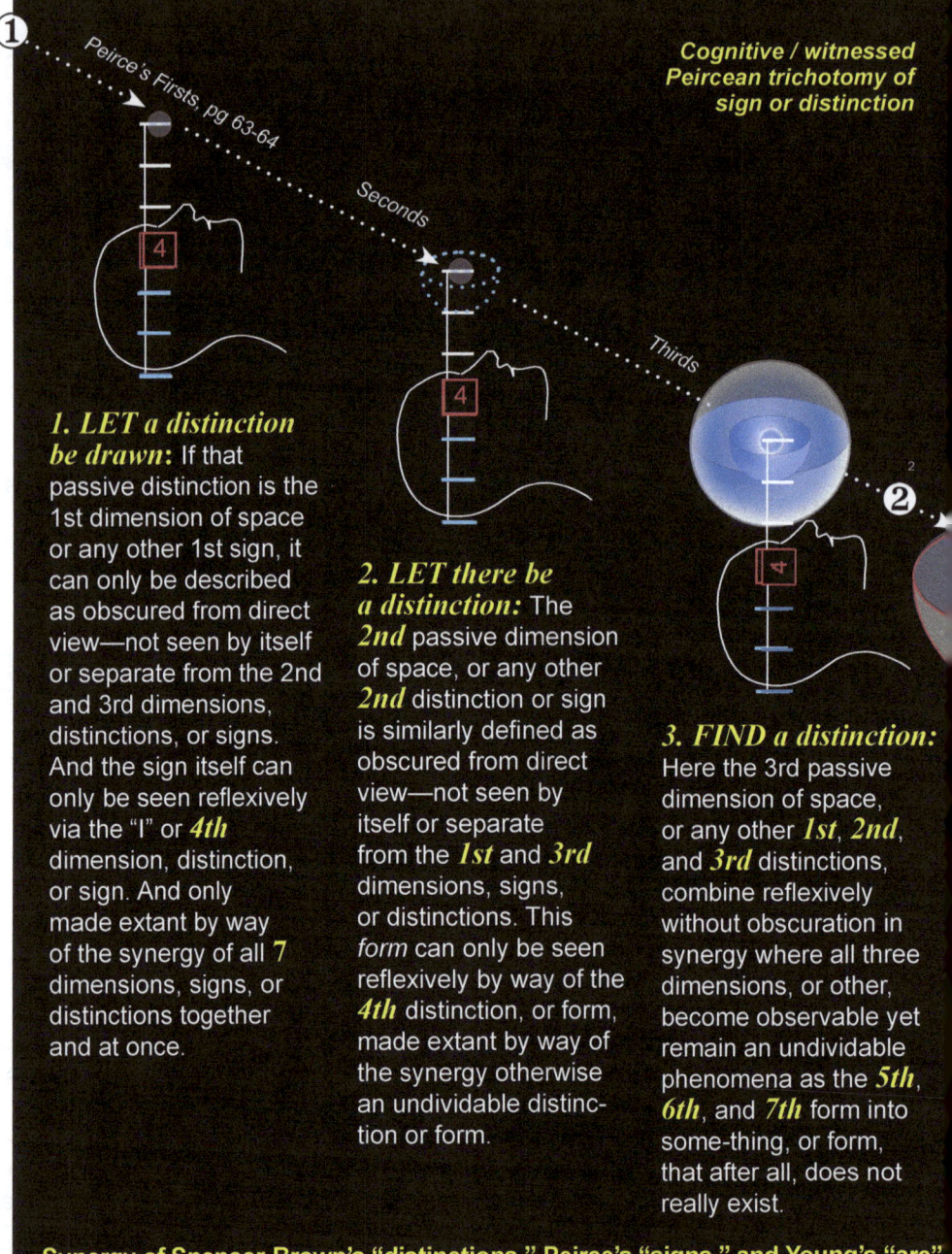

Peirce's Firsts, pg 63-64
Seconds
Thirds

Cognitive / witnessed
Peircean trichotomy of
sign or distinction

1. LET a distinction be drawn: If that passive distinction is the 1st dimension of space or any other 1st sign, it can only be described as obscured from direct view—not seen by itself or separate from the 2nd and 3rd dimensions, distinctions, or signs. And the sign itself can only be seen reflexively via the "I" or *4th* dimension, distinction, or sign. And only made extant by way of the synergy of all *7* dimensions, signs, or distinctions together and at once.

2. LET there be a distinction: The *2nd* passive dimension of space, or any other *2nd* distinction or sign is similarly defined as obscured from direct view—not seen by itself or separate from the *1st* and *3rd* dimensions, signs, or distinctions. This *form* can only be seen reflexively by way of the *4th* distinction, or form, made extant by way of the synergy otherwise an undividable distinction or form.

3. FIND a distinction: Here the 3rd passive dimension of space, or any other *1st*, *2nd*, and *3rd* distinctions, combine reflexively without obscuration in synergy where all three dimensions, or other, become observable yet remain an undividable phenomena as the *5th*, *6th*, and *7th* form into some-thing, or form, that after all, does not really exist.

Synergy of Spencer-Brown's "distinctions," Peirce's "signs," and Young's "arc"

[1] Consider the upper left margin of this panel to be "unmarked space," or the "boundary between everything and nothing," Dible's paper pp.63, re: Spencer-Brown's calculus in LoF.

Acquiring Mind — THE metasphere

REFLEXIVELY RE-COGNIZED IN THE CONATIVE OR ACTIVE SIDE OF MIND

Conative / reflexive Peircean trichotomy of sign or distinction

Firsts
Seconds
Reflex of Thirds

5. DESCRIBE a distinction: The tendency to separate out any category of ideas (e.g. space) into three states or signs, that apparently are not observable except in some prior unseparated, or unsevered state.

6. DEFINE a distinction: The impulse to form a relation, however obscure, between one dimension or other (of space), even if neither can be observed (seen or sensed) separately or such relation is even illusory to begin with.

7. DRAW a distinction: The unavoidable act or reflexive outcome of having "let" distinctions be drawn in the *1st* and *2nd* place —an act of synthesis that provides the necessary synergy for the reflexive apprehension of the three-dimensions of space, or apprehension of any other category of form or category[3] of ideas or of thinking in its usual biased or conative mode.

4. SEE a distinction: *"... a universe comes into being when a space is severed or taken apart. ...by tracing such severance, we can begin to see how the familiar laws of our own experience follow inexorably from the original act of severance. [That] universe cannot be distinguished from how we act upon it."* - G. Spencer-Brown, LoF, Pg XXIX

Before turning the page, replace the word "space" with "time" and re-read.

[2] The Arc of Process [mind], p.70, Arthur M. Young. LoF 1972 ed, p.103: "An observer, since [s]he distinguishes the space [s]he occupies, is also a mark." [4] "We must also indicate where the observer is supposed to be in relation to the expression." [3] Roget's categories of ideas, p.73. pp.106-105.

"The underlying and ubiquitous substratum of creation from nothing" R.D., p.63

The legend to the panel on the preceding spread-pages
by the author

The dimensions of *space* are by no means the extent to which, this *model*, this *metagraph*, this *metasphere*, applies. It is the *"underlying substratum"* [1] in which all thought comes to mind.

Notice the *"peculiar"* current or flow from the **passive,** or merely (cognitive) witnessing *appearance* side of mind, to the **active,** or definitive (conative) *apprehension* or **re-cognition** of that *appearance* now in the form or a set of distinctions.

Notice that there is no *appearance (of the "I")* except after the "I" [4] arises and acts upon, or reflexively *apprehends* its own appearance.

Notice the (arrowed dotted) lines of *perspective* emanating from the "I" *(that first person)* at the heart [4] of the model, and its resemblance to the *Deictic model* [2] with its *pointing* out to either side of the "I." However, in the *metaspheric model*, the lines reflexively point back toward the "self," vanishing into that apparent self (or "I.").

Notice the *cognitive* perspective (1-3) is about what is *not-self.* It is the *other*, or *second person*, while the *conative* (4-7) is necessarily what self does with that in-*form*-ation, *seen* from the point of view of the *"I,"* or *self*, or first person [4].

To the point of this paper, mind *reflexively* assumes a *predisposed knowing* or predisposed *apprehension* (7, 6, 5) which prior to its *apprehension* (1, 2, 3) is not a knowing at all, but passive or merely witnessed *appearance.* That predisposition is implicit in *drawing a distinction (7), defining it (6),* and *describing it (5),* because it affectively is a *metaspheric perspective* or the *point-of-view* of the *"I"* or *"self"* [4]. Thus, the scientist here will have a *scientific bias;* the philosopher, a *philosophical bias; and* the mystic, a predisposed *mystical point of view.*

So too, every other reader, consciously or unconsciously, has a *self-interest* or *self-purpose* in *mind* while apprehending appearance.

The metagraph[4] summarily models the everyday, moment-to-moment process around each and every particle or sign of information that comes (arises) to mind. In any single hour of the day, this process is repeated thousands even hundreds of thousands of times. However, the task, (the work,) is to take advantage of the gap or *nullpoint* [3] prior to the "I" becoming mind or viewpoint and those 4 to 7 distinctions.

Keep this virtual headgear in mind as you read on.

"What is"

---

[1] Dible, p.63. [2] p.49. [3] Nullpoint, p.76. [4] Previous page.

Arthur M. Young is one of the three principal outliers whose work supports this model of mind or *metapheric perspective,* providing the necessary dynamic "turn" or "arc," so important in modeling the *reflexive mechanism* of mind. He starts by explaining his *Cycle of Action* in phenomenological or experiential terms:

*"The start of the learning cycle (fig 1) is blind action: the infant reaches out at (1) and touches the hot stove, and at (2) reacts. Then at (3) he considers what has occurred; he becomes conscious that hot stoves hurt (if you are a behaviorist you can say he associates the pain with the stove), then at (4) he avoids the hot stove... This is the point of **conscious choice**. It makes possible the "turn,"... it is the entry of consciousness into the universe. ...**conscious action** merges back into (1) as avoidance becomes instinctive."*

— The Reflexive Universe, pg 266-267 [My brackets]

That *"avoidance"* not only *"becomes instinctive,"* but, I would add: that over eons of evolutionary time it became the entire explanation for the conative or *reflexive mind* — I would also say thus having lost any resemblance to a ***"conscious choice."***

This would equally apply to Young's *arc* in his *Arc of Process*—and I say this with less apology than Young (see below) for my attempt to explain:

"The 'turn' is the most important point of the whole arc, and while we cannot completely explain it, it is essential that we make room for it in our theory."[5]

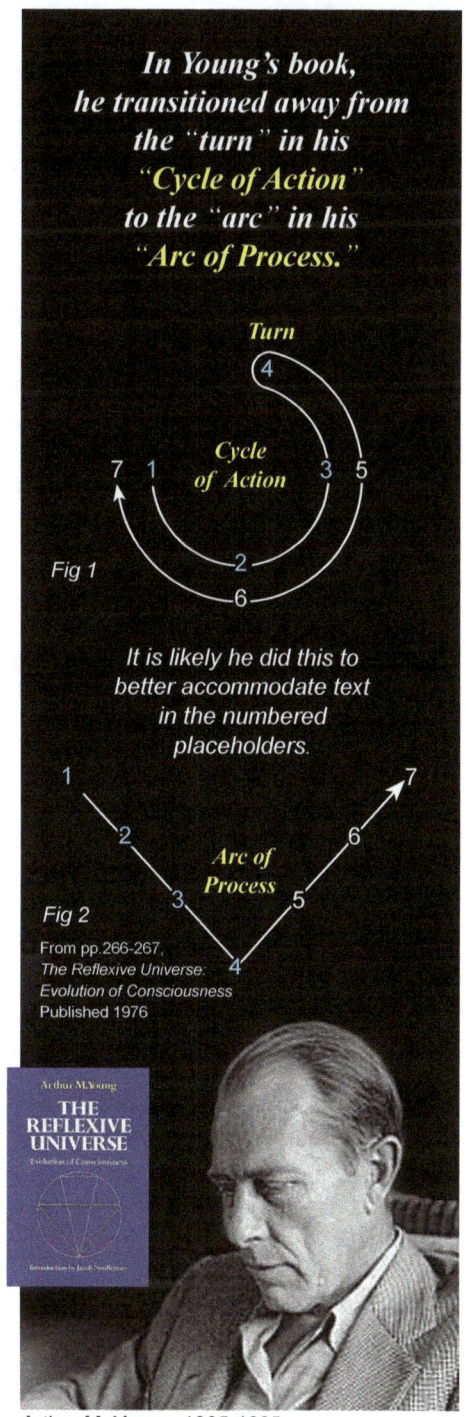

In Young's book, he transitioned away from the "turn" in his "Cycle of Action" to the "arc" in his "Arc of Process."

Fig 1

It is likely he did this to better accommodate text in the numbered placeholders.

Fig 2
From pp.266-267, The Reflexive Universe: Evolution of Consciousness Published 1976

Arthur M. Young, 1905-1995

[5] Young.

Another apparent apology by Young, which I heartily share:

"The intelligent reader is likely to regard with suspicion a theory that bases itself on the number seven. Legend, myth, fairy tales and superstitions have given it a bad reputation. My first contact with the occurrence of this number in ancient cosmologies affected me similarly. However, when I realized that topology, a science that deals with even more profound implications than does geometry, could supply formal reasons for a sevenfold ordering, I was prodded into a rethinking of the concepts embedded in relativity whose theories of curved space-time had provided the foundations for modern speculation on the nature of the universe."

"The evidence for seven stages to process found reinforcement from my study of nature; in the case of atoms, the periodic table showing seven rows; in the case of molecules, seven orders of combinations, and so on... Imagine my excitement to discover that... for projective geometry seven postulates were required." —Reflexive Universe, pp. 259 -268

My having found Young's work came out of an anxious search for a better way to justify or substantiate the intuitive tweak *(turn)* that I had given Peirce's trichotomy in applying it not only to the *cognitive side* of the model, but reflexively inverting it on the *conative side* as well *(pp.58-59)*. I searched for any use of the word "reflex' or *"reflexive"* in regard to mind and consciousness.

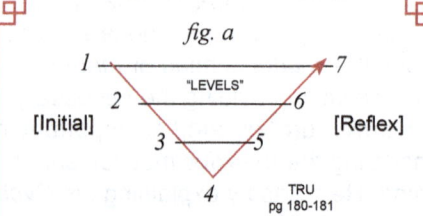

fig. a

Young's application of his Arc of Process

Young eventually points to what he calls *"correspondences"* between: 1 & 7, 2 & 6, and 3 & 5 of his "levels." Or in metaspheric parlance, the reflexive confluence between the cognitive and conative trichotomies of *sign*. Young intuited "fourthness" or that critical *turn* of mind.

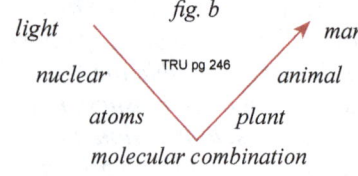

fig. b

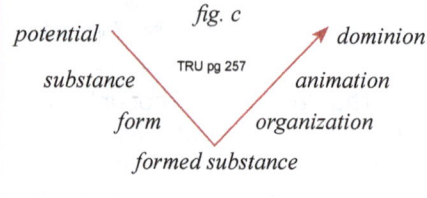

fig. c

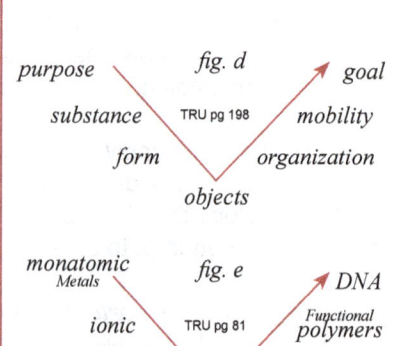

fig. d

fig. e

And coming across his book in 1977, **The Reflexive Universe**: *Evolution of Consciousness*, seemed a most astonishing find. Here, unlike Peirce, was a contemporary author, alive and well, who by the way, published another book around the same time, titled *The Geometry of Meaning*, and earlier, founded the Institute for the Study of Consciousness, in Berkeley, CA.

A man of like mind, he too gets into the mystery at the root of the number *seven*, which is its *septenary* symmetry, not its simple enumeration.

Young reminds us that in atomic physics the number of orbital spheres (electron shells) in an atom start at 1 in the lighter elements, and max out at 7 in the heavier elements, as do periods or the rows in the *Periodic Table of Elements*. Why this is, I am sure, the physicist has no real explanation. So too, a metaphysicist, like me, might say the same about *metaspheric thought*. Although as a phenomenologist, I can explain it as a principle that I am calling *septenary symmetry*, otherwise exemplified in the septenary structure of the energy of consciousness that I identified in *PartOne*, as Kundalini-Shakti.

"Most emphatic in its insistence on seven-ness is the ancient Hindu tradition.* In any case, I now had hint, perhaps a directive, that process involves seven stages." ... The periodic table, in fact was unequivocal in its support of the theory, for it divided all atoms into seven "periods" which show as the rows of the table itself." —Arthur M. Young,, TRU, pg xx & xxiii

---

* I am not sure, but I believe Young is referring to a "septenary perspective" in Hindu Jainism called:

Anekantavada or Saptabhanginaya:
1. *It is what is*
2. *It is not what is*
3. *It is what is and not*
4. ***It is what is indefinite***
5. *It is what is and indefinite*
6. *It is what is not and indefinite*
7. *It is what is, is not, and indefinite*

Like Spencer-Brown, Young's research was at so many levels, and with influences so complex that he (also like Roget[1]) found it intuitively necessary to put his findings into the *fewest categories* possible, which for both, apparently and apprehensively, is seven.

The result of using the *"levels"* on his *Arc of Process*, he called "The Grid,"

	Potential	Binding	Identity	Combination	Growth	Mobility	Consciousness
1. LIGHT *(Potential)*	10^{21} Hz	10^{22} Hz	10^{18} Hz	10^{15} Hz	10^{11} Hz	10^{9} Hz	10^{4} Hz
	Spectrum of electromagnetic radiation from Gamma rays to Low frequency Radio waves						
2. NUCLEAR *(Binding)*	In Young's time it was called "Quantum Probability Fog."						
	[Today, particle physicists have a 3-ring "Standard Model,"]						
3. ATOMIC *(Identity)*	Periodic table of Elements:						
	Row 1 H^1-He^2	Row 2 Li^3-Ne^{10}	Row 3 Na^{11}-Ar^{18}	Row 4 K^{19}-Kr^{36}	Row 5 Rb^{37}-Xe^{54}	Row 6 Cs^{55}-Rn^{86}	Row 7 Fr^{87}-Uuo^{118}
4. MOLECULAR *(Combination)*	Metals 1 atom	Ionic Salts 2 atoms	Paraffin Series Compounds	Functional Series Compounds	Polymers Cell Chains	Proteins Side Chains	DNA and Viruses Replicating
5. PLANT *(Growth)*	Bacteria 1cell	Algae 1-tissue	Embryo-phytes 1-tissue Coelen-	Psiophy-tales n-tissue	Gymno-sperms seeds	Gymno-sperms seeds	Angio-sperms flowers
6. ANIMAL *(Mobility)*	Protozoa 1 cell	Sponges n cells	terates 1 organ	Mullusks- n-organ	Annelids n-chains	Arthropods n-chains	Chordata vertebrates
7. DOMINION* *(Consciousness)*	?	Tribal Collective Unconscious	Self- Consciousness	Modern Man Objective Thought	---> Creative Thought	Realized Personages i.e. Buddha	?

is a taxonomy of the descent of *light* into inorganic and organic matter, with an inverse upturn precisely at the 4th or *molecular* level. All told, he traces in complex detail seven stages and sub-stages of the "evolution of *consciousness*[2] *[mind]."* It also seems Young's intrigue was to apply the *"Arc"* in myth, as well as science.

A distinction to be made in *metaspheric perspective* is that consciousness is "what is" unchanged, whereas *mind* does indeed evolve and has been *repurposed* many times in its hundreds of thousands of years of evolution.

---

[1] Roget, p.73.   [1] Subtitle of Young's book *The Reflexive Universe* p.69.

> The words consciousness and mind are often used interchangeably, so it seems definitions are necessary.
>
> ## *A glossary of terms:*
>
> **mind**: *Flow or stream of signs as words, the information you are somehow hearing in your head.*
> **consciousness**: *Flow itself, without information or definition, prior, during, and after mind.*
> **flow:** *To derive from a source or move with continual change of place, as does mind, but not necessarily consciousness.*
> **current:** *That direction of the flow of information from the cognitive to the conative side of mind.*[1]
> **reflexive:** *The "current" as non linear, a turnabout,*[2] *where the "I" unavoidable or evolutionarily focuses all information onto itself.*
> **self:** *Predisposed perspective, point-of-view or "knowing" based on the evolutionary "reflex" of mind.*[3]
> **bias:** *That reflex, that leaning or predisposition through the median or point-of-view of the "I."*[3]
> **purpose:** *In the context of mind, the logic or mechanism active as bias or predisposition.*
> **repurpose:** *To accept and make alternate use of the unavoidable or evolutionary force of the present purpose of mind.*
> **metagraph:** *Any graphic that incorporates both word and graphic, especially in reference to presenting an idea or thought process.*
> **metasphere:** *The author's name for a particular metagraph limning the reflexive model of mind.*

Although **Peter Mark Roget** is best known for the *Roget's Thesaurus* sitting on your bookshelf, he was more than a lexicographer, he was a physician, metaphysician, inventor, and certainly a phenomenologist. He left us with this remarkable insight in his introduction to his original 1852 thesaurus.

"Metaphysicians are agreed that scarcely any of our intellectual operations could be carried on to any considerable extent without the agency of words. Words are the instruments [signs] by which we form all our abstractions, by which we fashion and embody our ideas, and by which we are enabled to glide along a series of premises and conclusions with rapidity so great as to leave in the memory no trace of the successive steps of the process; and we remain unconscious how much we owe to this potent auxiliary..."[PMR] [My bracket]

Roget's insight certainly echoes Lowe's thesis around the *"acquisition of language"* and Peirce's *"Thought-Signs."* Yet, I would argue with Roget, where he says *"...no trace of the successive steps in the process."* The steps may not be in *"memory,"* but they have, at last, been made conscious here in the model by way of a phenomenological method, which puts into a snapshot that *"rapidity"* of thought, slowed down to a stop-action frame in metaspheric perspective of all seven *"successive steps in the process."*

Roget also had an intuition of the number of categories of words, and applied it in the outline or synopsis of categories in his original 1852 thesaurus:

---

[1] Panels: p.58-59, 66-67, 78-79. [2] Young's Arc of Process [Mind], pp.69-71. [3] Especially p.78-79.

Acquiring Mind   THE SEVEN CATEGORIES OF IDEAS   73

Excerpt from the Introduction, pages x to xi, 1852 edition of his thesaurus.
[My brackets, 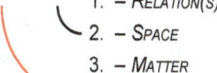, and underlines]

Roget's order and number of categories of ideas or words relate to the septenary symmetry of mind [metasphere]:

    1. – RELATION(S)

"**The first** of these [categories] comprehends ideas derived from more general and ABSTRACT RELATIONS among things, such as Existence, Resemblance, Quantity, Order, Number, Time, Power.

    1. – RELATION(S)
    2. – SPACE

The second refers to SPACE and its various relations, including Motion or change of place.

    1. – RELATION(S)
    2. – SPACE
    3. – MATTER

The third includes ideas that relate to the MATERIAL WORLD, namely the Properties of Matter ...as well as the Perceptions to which it gives rise.

    1. – RELATION(S)
    2. – SPACE
    3. – MATTER
    4. – INTELLECTION

Note how Roget's category of "intellection" corresponds to the "I" [4] point-of-view, or the "self."

"**The fourth** embraces all ideas of phenomena relating to INTELLECT and its operation ...the Acquisition, Retention, and Communication of ideas."

Peter Mark Roget
1779-1869

    1. – RELATION(S)
    2. – SPACE
    3. – MATTER
    4. – INTELLECTION
    5. – VOLITION

The fifth includes the ideas derived from the exercise of VOLITION, embracing the phenomena and results of our Voluntary and Active Powers.

    1. – RELATION(S)
    2. – SPACE
    3. – MATTER
    4. – INTELLECTION
    5. – VOLITION
    6. – AFFECTIONS

The sixth comprehends all ideas derived from the operation of our [AFFECTIONS] SENTIMENT AND MORAL POWERS, including our Feelings, Emotions, Passions, and Moral and Religious Sentiments."

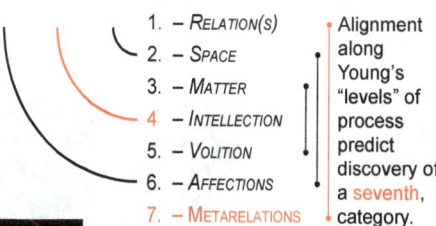

    1. – RELATION(S)
    2. – SPACE
    3. – MATTER
    4. – INTELLECTION
    5. – VOLITION
    6. – AFFECTIONS
    7. – METARELATIONS

Alignment along Young's "levels" of process predict discovery of a seventh, category.

The Seventh category of words, (ideas) is predicted by the model, thus not necessarily in Roget's mind. Whereas the category is the necessary leap or the meta-extention of his first category.

Also see Tribute to Roget, pp. 106-107.

We cannot leave Roget's work without pairing his *"signification"* or "the idea [word] is intended to convey" with Peirce's idea of *"signhood."* [My bracket]

*"Signhood is a way of **being in relation**, not a way of being in itself. Anything is a sign — not as itself, but in some relation or other."* – Peirce / Wikipedia.

We also cannot leave Young's *"Arc of Process"* without mentioning his intrigue with myth as well as science. He devotes a whole chapter to it, titled:

Process as described in myth*:*
"Science, in fact, has become so fragmented into separate disciplines that it has lost sight of the unifying principle that the word 'universe' implies. ...accounts in myth and legend, seemingly naive, have an amazing sense of wholeness, ... science, like a map, can furnish information, but it cannot provide a compass. Myth supplies this compass."

My own intrigue with myth has been with some of its metagraphics and artifacts that apparently echo the same axis of symmetry discovered in the metaspheric model of mind.

The Symmetry in Myth

Young's interest was not confined to the scientific disciplines, and as an expositor, he was willing to explore:

"the myths of cosmology ... In many of these accounts, process is described as occurring in seven stages... God makes the universe in six days and rests on the seventh... So too the Zoroastrian and the Japanese accounts." -TRU, p xx, xxiii

This 400 year old frontispiece has had many different interpretations. One, that the author offers, is its remarkable resemblance to an inverted metasphere and the *"conscious choice"* that Young refers to. Note the chain ❶ of *appearance,* and on the *other hand* ❹ , the *choice* to release or drop egoic *"apprehension"* of that mere appearance ❼ .

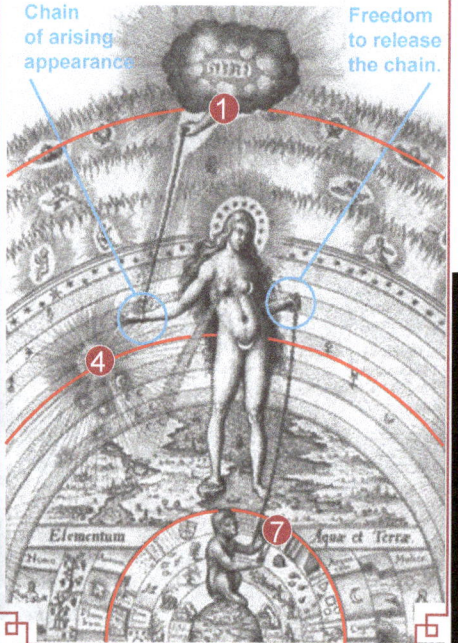

Chain of arising appearance
Freedom to release the chain.

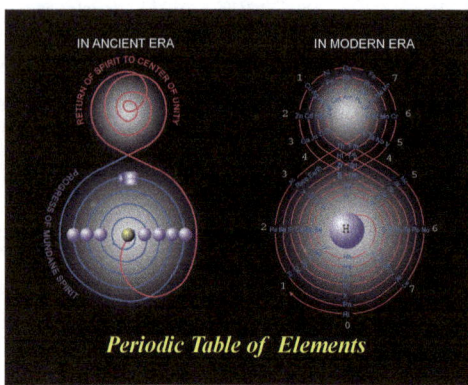

IN ANCIENT ERA IN MODERN ERA

Periodic Table of Elements

Path of Sacred Scarab.   Seven periodic levels.   1617 book frontispiece: Mirror of the Whole of Nature.

Arthur M. Young's *"arc"* or *turn of mind* is well demonstrated in our model[1] and in myth. However, it is not, as he called it, *"the entry of consciousness,"*[2] for consciousness has been there all along in the premonitory *"**nullpoint**"*[3] prior to *"the entry of mind (the "I")."* Such a *nullstate* is symbolized as the orb between the opposing prongs of *phenomenon* and *noumenon,* in the Tibetan Buddhist ceremonial implement called the *Vajra or Dorje*[4] *(lightening bolt).* I have taken artistic license in the remaining images *(below)* to show how a **nullstate** might be recognized across the board in similar mystical and scientific metagraphs.

The *metaspheric model* represents **seven states** in the reality-separating process that mind performs every moment— even as convergence remains the background against which that *separating-out* is apparently accomplished. It seems that mind took an evolutionary **fork in the road**, splitting off its separative function from its non-separative state, that of *Consciousness*[5] itself. What possible test of the accuracy of our model is there other than to test drive it yourself?

You will have that opportunity in *PartThree*. So, get ready to put on the *booting up headgear*[6] provided and get behind the wheel of a *metapheric perspective scenario.*

Here in the last few pages of *PartTwo,* direct your attention to the code in metaspheric perspective, which I call the *"nullpoint.*[3]*"* During the test drive it is necessary to remember that point, and to realize that the model is not linear, rather a *quantum construct,* subject to the *probabilistic* conditions, comparable to the difficulty particle physicists have—a construct with single cars in the continuum [of mind] that will regularly go off the rails, particularly, given any quantum arc. Like the model of a proton, called the *"Standard Model,"*[7] with its *"probabilistic cloud"* of 17 particles, we can only take into account the **probable** location in space-time of any single particle [or sphere in our temporal *metaspheric model* of mind]. Thus, similar intuition and accommodation is to be given our *metaspheric perspective,* just as we would give the physicists' perspective of matter.

Ancient and modern models of metaspheric perspective hint at a nullpoint or nullstate in the process.

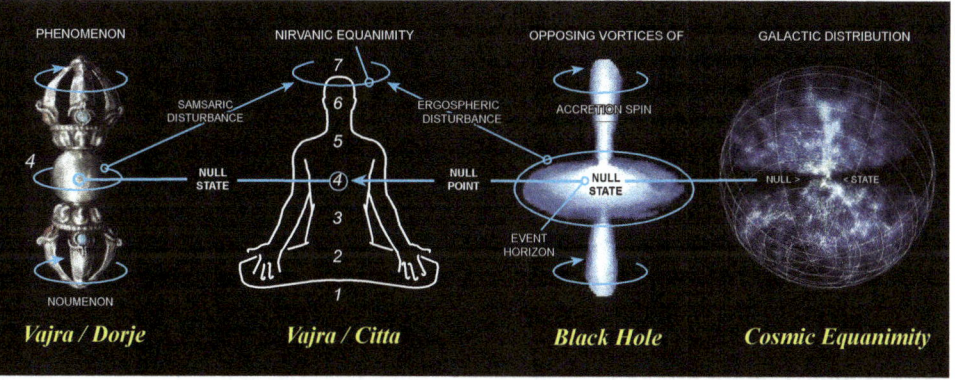

Biblio. Circle of Bliss, Pg 223,   PartOne Pg 41   Artist's Rendering   6dF Galaxy Survey

---

[1] pp.66-67.   [2] Young.   [3] ParOne p.23.   [4] Vajra/Dorje .   [5] Glossary p.72.   [6] p.61, pp.64-65.

Having in mind the phenomenological territory that our group of outliers discovered, You end up with a *model* of mind not unlike a *map,*[1] which could only have been drawn or observed from some point above or transcendent to both map and the territory, which the map models—which is to acknowledge a premonitory "You" that neither inhabits the *map* nor the *territory*—a "You" that is not of mind, rather of Consciousness. And like *"presence,*[2]*"* is neither "self" nor "other," which is where the *"**nullpoint**"* [3] comes in—after *appearance* but before *conative*[4] *apprehension* of that *cognitive*[4] *appearance.*

Understandably, the *nullpoint* is not directly observable, for if it were, it would then be a **viewpoint** *(the "I" point-of-view).*[5] Yet, its existence is *predicted* in the calculus of the model. And although this *nullpoint* is void, it is that instance of nothing happening that provides the escapement mechanism to counter the purpose of mind—that evolutionary *bias* favoring self-interest and preservation of self.

Consider the *nulling* effect that the *escapement anchor* in a clockwork provides, which makes the clock hand *click* forward, not simply *spin* out of control. As a kid, I took apart an old windup alarm clock, and removed the escapement anchor.[6] And as a harmless prank I hid the bare clockwork of spinning gears in a paper bag, letting the raspy sound of the gears against the inside of the bag astonish my friends on the school bus. Remarkably, that portion of energy spent between the escapement cog has an equivalency to the energy in a portion of the spin. This is the **dynamic constant** prior to mind.

The *nullpoint* is not a forestalling of the spin of mind, rather a mere *point* in the *process* where a conscious choice can be made *toward repurposing* the spin *of mind.* No force within mind can defeat mind, but mind itself can be repurposed. What can be done is to remember that the escapement point exists, and somewhere, in the "arc" or "turn" in the spin (process) of mind, acknowledge and deflect, as best "You" can, away from "self" and toward "other." Do this enough and "You" eventually realize that there is no real difference between the three[7].

Just as the *nullpoint* is vanished by the "I," the "I" is vanished an equal number of times by the *"nullpoint."* A "nullstate" is exemplified when we are "un-conscious," a condition that according to the understanding of Consciousness here, would be more accurately, and simply, termed unmindful. Which is to say that mind is *discontinuous* and Consciousness is *constant,* unmodified by the artifacts apprehended in mind or on the *map.* Where there is merely flow, that is *Consciousness.* Where there is that artifactual content, that is *mind.*

Recall that in *Part-One,* several other *flow-events* spontaneously arose, there too, not in mind, but in Consciousness: **"Presence, surrender, and bliss"** all were initiated at the technical *turn or "arc"* in the *model* and identified now as the *nullpoint* on the median,[8] phenomenologically corresponding to the *"affectual mode"* between the *cognitive* mode and *conative* mode of mind. This *median* place is where the *work* is done, but not by means available to the "I."

---

[1] pp.66-67, 78-79. [2] pp.20-21. [3] p.23, p.68 [pp.82-83]. [4] p.58-59. [5] p.79. [6] clockwork. [7] You, yourself, and the other. [8] Panel, p.78-79, dotted circle is the median between cognitive and conative mind.

Another allusion to the *nullpoint* is the phrase **The Razor's Edge,** an analogue that Somerset Maugham used in his novel by the same name. He in turn took it from a line in the Vedic *Katha Upanishad,* which in turn is translated here with metaspheric license:

[The nullpoint] ...like the Razor's Edge, it is not possible to tread for long without the "I" and accompanying predisposed mechanisms of mind becoming operative and all manner of bias bleeding through uninspected without a second or afterthought.[9]

As sharp as it is, this razor's edge, there are means to make better use of its cutting edge. Meditation is often thought of as that means, to cut through mind, yet it is not the "I" (itself) that can do that, for **the "I" itself is mind**. Also, to refer to meditation as if it were some standardized means is likewise misleading; especially meditation of that *self-initiated* kind, which puts at odds the notion of *presence*—that *no-self, no-other* or *"nullstate"*—or instance of *no-mind*.

There is then spontaneous meditation by which "**You**" (not the "I") cuts through mind, which, again, implies a distinction between C̲onsciousness (the "You") and mind (the "I" consciousness). So, who are You? The nagging intuition 50 years ago and still today, is that "You" are that C̲onsciousness that is neither *map* nor *territory,* rather the *nullstate*— pristine C̲onsciousness in which *surrender* is spontaneously located, but cannot be searched for. The meditation, the work, is to simply live with the model in mind, be in the company of those who have located the *nullpoint,* by no means of the "I," and lean into it repeatedly.

Remember the *"**unmarked space**"*[2] mentioned in Spencer-Brown's *LoF?* That is pristine Consciousness prior to *marking* (distinguishing) the metaspheric perspective of the *"I," self,* or *mind.*

The realization, then, is that the first, primus, or primordial state of who or what "You" are prior to the "I" or self" is *surrender itself,* simply *awareness.* Even the word awareness alone may not be enough to say. That is why Buddhism qualifies *awareness* with the modifier *"pristine,"* as in the following:

*"**Appearances** originating in primordial [a priori] consciousness are the spontaneous, natural effulgence of pristine awareness.* **Being neither the mind nor mental processes,** *'these appearances are by nature the play of the manifest space of awareness —dharmadhatu.*[10]*"*

– B. Alan Wallace, Stilling the Mind, 2011 [My brackets].

In *PartOne,* I describe *"The Surrender Event*[11] and the immediate effect of that spontaneous giving-up as the appearance of *Presence,* followed by *apprehension* of an *effulgence* or love-bliss, which, in reality, may be the only direct **non-reflexive** mode of mind— that *"affectual"* mode.

And given that pleasurable enfolding comfort of *Presence,* it is more evident than we think that such *feelingly* observable *"signs"* like those in the neuroception *(Kundalini)* processes—*signs* most often called mystic experience: the *feeling of being, bliss, love, merging,* and *disillusion,* and certainly the *feeling release* of *Surrender,* are to be expected as part of the movement *toward repurposing mind.* Perhaps only in that affectual mode[12] of mind is the *conative* mode put out of its misery.

---

[9] [PartThree p.89]. [10] Skt. dhatu, space or sphere of dharma "absolute reality." [11] pp.20-23, 36. [12] p.59.

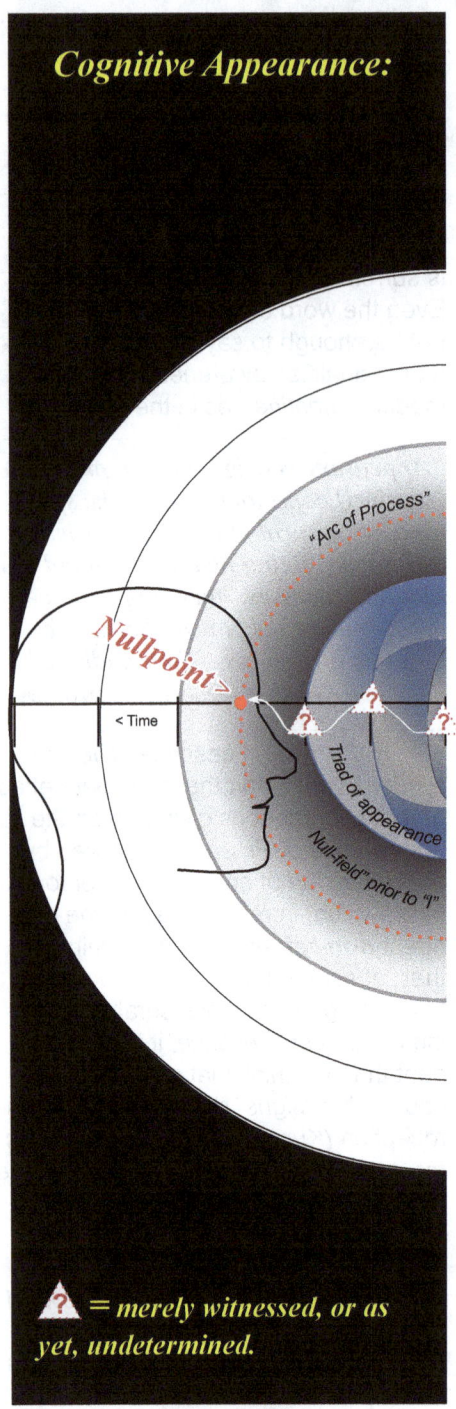

Cognitive Appearance:

⚠ = *merely witnessed, or as yet, undetermined.*

It is in that *affectual*[1] mode between the *cognitive* and *conative* sides of mind that the *nullpoint* is posited as a *point* in the *arc of process* immediately after the triad of a cognitive *appearance* but prior to the arising of the "I" and conative *apprehension* of that *appearance*. It is at this very heart of metaspheric perspective that the **nullpoint**, just prior to the *turn* or *"arc,*[2]*"* of mind is shown here on the *verso page*. The *recto page* shows the **viewpoint**, or what happens after cognitive appearance ❓ has been *apprehended* by the "I" ⚠, — after the "I" is already in the game.

Once the *nullpoint* is vanished by *viewpoint,* there is no re-turning to it, no chance for spontaneous *Presence (no self, no other)*—that necessary precursor to *repurposing mind* in that particular *metaspheric cycle of thought.*

On the other hand, "You" have a lifetime remaining of metaspheric cycles of *appearance,* each coming to mind in their own Peircean[3] and Brownean[4] form, each with their *gap* or *nullpoint* and potential for *"subordinating"* the evolutionary bias of self, self-interests, and self-preservation.

If mind were a game, mastery of the *"Game"* would require someone *"...cultivated enough to subordinate"*[5] conative apprehension of cognitive appearance, with the least level of modifying bias slipping through.

In one's ordinary thought and in conversation with another, this would look like *deflecting* a rigid stance in yourself and in another. It might be described to a friend as taking advantage of a rare moment of hearing both sides of the mental chatter—like a distant radio talk show, nothing to do with "YOU."

This metagraph is an alternate to the one on pp.66-67, using the same "headgear." [1] Modularity of mind pp.58-59.   [2] Young pp.66-67.   [3] Peirce pp.54-55.   [4] Brown pp.62-63.   [5] Hesse p.82.

Acquiring Mind

To put all this in some transitional context or see how far the "I" of "You" has come, look back at a time when "You" had no *"metaspheric perspective,"* no *differentiated* mind.

"...a time when you [could not] distinguish between what is you and what is not you. ...a time [of undifferentiated oneness] before... one's acquisition of language."[6]

Or as Lowe summarized it:
"My radical idea is that consciousness [mind] is a construct of human language..."[6]   [My paraphrasing & brackets]

And now perhaps the reader is able to see beyond that *"Verbal curtain,"*[7] beyond the *"construct of human language,"*[6] especially if mind has made the ontological **distinction** between *mind* as *thinking* and that *C*onsciousness is simply *being*—limning that distinction between *viewpoint and nullpoint* is essentially metaspheric perspective.

In line with the conative impulse to "do" something about it, rather than simply "be," the directive is heard in the talking schools of non-duality, which is **"transcend the ego,"** the "I," the mind. This bit of "doing" begs a number of questions: Who or what is saying this and who or what is receiving this directive? Is it the *"differentiated one"*[6] telling *"undifferentiated consciousness"*[6]—non-dual reality talking to a duality? Either way, it is not merely rhetorically meaningless, but a fool's errand, since it presumes two entities, the "I" and God (Consciousness), whereas we have seen that at least one of those is not even an entity. And if we must "do" something, turn the page and **let's play a game**, one you may have heard of.

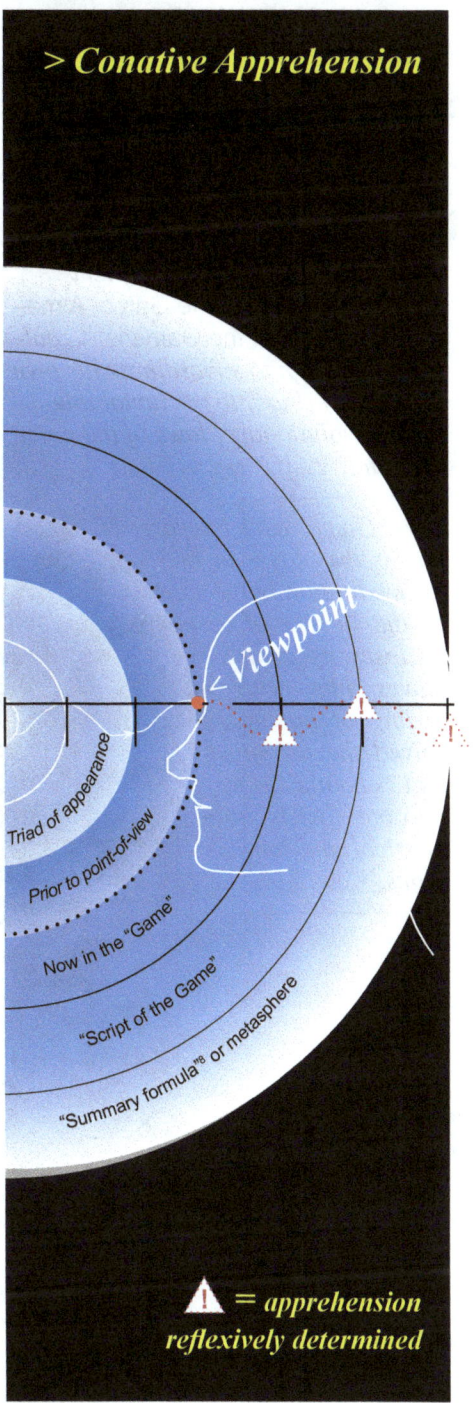

> *Conative Apprehension*

⚠ = *apprehension reflexively determined*

---

[6] Lowe, p.46-47.   [7] Leary, pp.50-51.   [4] Hesse, p.82.

In his 1946 Nobel Prize winning novel *Magister Ludi*, Hermann Hesse called it *The Glass Bead Game*. A game played in a 25th century pedagogic community in Europe called *Castalia*, where the *"Game"* has been taught and played for centuries.

Without calling it mastery of *mind*, Hesse uses the phrase *"mastery play"* as the goal of the Game. A magister (master) of the Game is: *"...cultivated enough to subordinate his own inspiration [bias] to the inviolable inner [evolutionary] laws of the game [of mind] itself."* _{GBG, [My brackets]}

"The Game, as I interpret it, encompasses the player at the conclusion of his meditation in the same way as the surface of a sphere encloses its centre, and leaves him with the feeling of having resolved the fortuitous and chaotic world into one that is symmetrical and harmonious." _{GBG, Magister Ludi}

Understandably, Hesse gives the reader no exact explanation of how the game is played, other than the excerpt that I have included on *page 82*, leaving it as enigmatic as *metasphere* may seem to some of my readers— each to infer their own explanation, and rules of play. And as Tim Leary says of Hesse's work and of *the GBG* in particular:

"Most readers miss the message of Hesse. Entranced by the pretty dance of plot and theme, they overlook the seed message ... the electrical message, the code..." — Timothy Leary, Politics of Ecstasy

Perhaps the next part of the book, this appropriating of Hesse's *Glass Bead Game*, this thought experiment, this tangible application of *PartTwo* will provide sufficient re-booting, repurposing, of mind that the *"the code, the message"* will be clearly seen. ◆

arising appearance

< self

reflexive turn toward self

Like glass beads, the spheres of mind are strung on the endless thread of Consciousness.

Part Three
Repurposing Mind

THE GAME MANUAL

THE APPLICATION OF METASPHERIC PERSPECTIVE

Our model[1] of metaspheric mind requires an esthetic as well as technical understanding, so perhaps in this last part of the book a playful and poetic approach is permitted. With what descriptions are given in Hesse's book, the Game could have as much promise as one might hope for our present civilization, in similar peril.

> *"The colored beads, his playthings, in his hand, He sits head bent; around him lies a land Laid waste by war and ravaged by disease."*[2]

As I am writing this part of the book, aside from the climate crisis, a war in Europe is raging and the Omicron Covid variant has spread—the even more immediate reminder that human biology, like the ecology of the planet, like civilization, is fragile. Yet, who is re-minded that it is *self-first* mind which is the real virus poisoning the climate, and the cause of war? Who is even willing to admit there is a climate crisis, much less their own *self-first* participation in it? I need only think of the pollution released into the atmosphere for my convenient transportation to the comfortable air conditioned grocery store and access to plenty of out-of-season fresh produce and refrigerated meats.

And who is *conscious* of the financial and political self-interests and conveniences that come at the expense of some other poor "self" on the planet.

Stuck at home during the pandemic quarantine, I saw a story on my social media news feed about anthropologist Margaret Mead who reportedly was asked what she considered the *first sign of civilization*: Mead repotedly replied[3] that such a sign was finding a fractured femur or thighbone from an individual who lived 12 thousand years ago. The fossilized bone showed definite signs of careful mending— mending that could not have happened without someone having the heroic dedication to tend to the injured person's immediate and long term needs. One can guess that a team of *caregivers* formed, and it is most likely that they were all women.

And who, in light of the pandemic hospital crisis, and mask debate, has not endured the *first sign of the fall of civilization?* It does not take an anthropologist nor phenomenologist to see the signs of an opposing *other-first* and *self-first* mentality. Certainly the *other-first* frame of mind is least demonstrated, thus the term "heroic," which results in burnout for *other-firsters* and passive aggression, even violence, from *self-firsters* toward *other-firsters*.

---

[1] Model, pp.78-79 and p.83. [2] See full quote p.94. [3] Attribution to Mead is unsubstantiated, however; the notion is relevant.

The *problem* is not that technology and invention brought about the climate crisis, and certainly the *promise* is not remedial technology and invention. The *problem* is the evolutionary *flaw*[1] in the very *purpose* of mind, its "self." And the *promise* is an entirely "other" civilization based on *re-purposing* the *purposed "self-first"* mind.

Unlike the slower *non-conscious* evolutionary changes to mind, for change to be immediate, there must be a *conscious* repurposing of mind—a moment to moment *first-person* examination of the "turn"[2] of mind to "self" that otherwise occurs without a "second thought"—*"without evaluating the validity of the initial thought."*[3]

By observing the process of mind in this way, as a string of beads or game pieces in play, one can plot the signs of thought in-form-ation—on the fly, so to speak. Mind cannot stand still for some leisurely examination. So, in the *Game* it is necessary to imagine every move of game pieces in stop-action, or slowed down to where a snapshot or stilling of the action can then be carefully examined, and when your *"turn"* comes, a *conscious* choice can be made.

The next two snippets from Hesse's *The Glass Bead Game* give a feel for how the *Game* was (is) played and will serve as a **crib sheet** for a present understanding of the play of mind:

> "... everyone is free to play the game privately... [public Games] take place under the leadership of a few superior Masters who are directly subordinate to the Ludi Magister, or Master of the Game...with invited guests listening raptly [in meditative mode]."

> "*He appeared in the festival hall in the midst of his many acolytes, conducting step after step of his Game... With a luminous golden stylus he delicately inscribed character after character on the small tablet before him, and the same characters promptly appeared in the script of the Game, enlarged a hundred fold, upon the gigantic board on the rear wall of the hall, to be spelled out by a thousand whispering voices, called out by the Speakers, broadcast to the country and the world. And when... he wrote the summary formula ... upon his tablet, ... gave instructions for the meditation, laid down the stylus and, taking his seat, assumed the perfect meditation posture... throughout Castalia and beyond, in many countries of the globe, the faithful devotees of the Glass Bead Game reverently sat down for the self same meditation and sustained it until the moment the Magister in the hall rose to his feet once again... The abstract and seemingly timeless world of the Game was flexible enough to respond, in a hundred nuances, to the mind, voice, temperament, and handwriting of a given personality, and the personality in this case was...cultivated enough to subordinate his own inspirations to the inviolable inner laws of the Game itself.*" -Hesse, The Glass Bead Game

As a tribute and courtesy to Hesse and his copyright, the Game has been renamed *Metasphere: The flaw in the play of mind*. In the cursory description of play *(above)* one gets the feeling that the Game had come to be performed with a sense of ceremony and *"delicacy;"* tracking *"character after character... in the script of the game"* to arrive at the *"summary formula"*— (metasphere).

---

[1] The "self-first" point of view. [2] Young pp.69-71. [3] Beck, pp.66-67.

Repurposing Mind THE gameboard 83

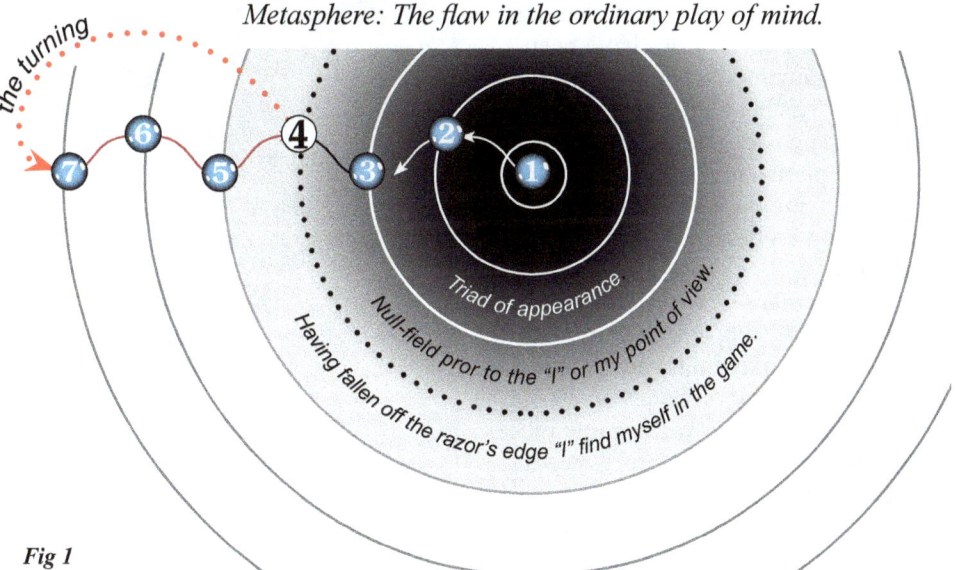

Fig 1

Imagine the Game board of mind on a "gigantic[4]" screen.

Today, in the midst of the crisis, there seems no place or time left for *"delicacy"* and *"sustained meditation.[4]"* Rather, one needs to resort to whatever means would expedite learning the Game—this *"flaw in the play of mind."*

Several curious tools are already suggested in Hesse's novel, written in 1945—familiar devices in present day use. Instead of the *"luminous golden stylus"* and *"small tablet,"* let's use a *smart phone and touch screen stylus.* And imagine there exists a downloadable game *app* named *(m)etasphere.*™

Now with internet and phone connection secured, we can see *"...the script of the Game enlarged a hundred fold, upon a gigantic monitor [board] on the rear wall of the hall, to be spelled out [on our individual smart phones] by a thousand [readers'] whispering voices, [pondering each play] ...broadcast to the country and the world."[4]*

Before proceeding, it is interesting to note the origin of the name *"Glass Bead Game."* Legend has it that it came about centuries before Castalia—a much different, less sophisticated, less subtle game than the one narrated in the snippet on the previous page:

"...a frame, modeled on a child's abacus, a frame with several dozen wires on which could be strung glass beads of various colors. The wires corresponded to the lines of a musical staff, the beads to the time values of the notes and so on. ...In technical terms this was a mere child's plaything. ...And as is often the case, an enduring and significant institution received its name from a passing and incidental circumstance." —Hesse, GBG

And perhaps it is the power given later to the glass beads as thought-signs *(like musical notation)* that make the name relevant to the play of mind today.

[4-5] Hesse-GBG snippet p.82. [Fig 1,] Gameboard with "signs" labeling the Glass Beads (spheres) in the unbroken thread (flow) of consciousness.

The *Game* has been played much longer than its rules have been documented. What documentation does exist[1] has been programmed into the *Game* app user-manual for upload to a smart phone and/or to a computer communicating with a monitor or projector. Use a stylus or finger tip to call up tutorials and/or enter resulting *scripts* of any particular *Game play*.

Figures 1-6 unpack here the same *Game rules* of play that were depicted in an alternate way on *pages 66-67* and *78-79*—along with how the game pieces *(thought-signs embedded in glass beads)* move and the significance of their position in *metaspheric perspective*. The summary text below the screenshots would otherwise appear on screen along with other explanatory callouts.

Fig 2 shows the *home screen* or, in Eastern logic, the depth and flow of Pristine Consciousness ● and, in Western logic, Spencer-Brown's **Unmarked State** [2] posited in his *Laws of Form and* prior to the *"First Distinction,*[2]*" form* or sign of *appearance*.

Fig 3 shows *"First Distinction,*[3]*" marked space, or sign* which Peircean logic unpacks as a trichotomy[4] of *appearance,* represented on screen as bead *Game pieces* ◉◉◉— coincident with their respective placeholder spheres ◉ of *passive-cognitive* consciousness, which, like the beads, spontaneously emerge differentiated from the depth of undifferentiated Consciousness.

Fig 4 shows the *median* ◉ placeholder in consciousness for the ***apparent** "**I**," observer,* or *interpreter sign,*[4] ④ coincident with the potential signs of *passive* appearance ◉, which can eventually be named ①②③ anticipating their conative (reflexive) apprehension.

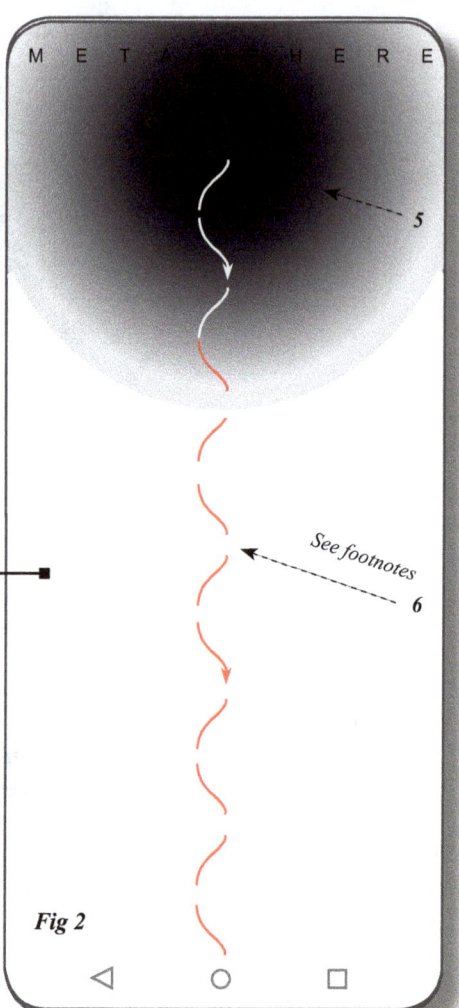

Fig 2

The "Unmarked Space" [7]

Prior to the start of the game, there is only the undifferentiated space ● and flow ⟿ of Consciousness, no sign ◯ of thought, no content ③, no "I," no self ④, no other; merely witnessed presence. Of course at some point the game unavoidable starts with a **first distinction** or sign of appearance— bead of thought, a word, anticipating apprehension of that appearance.

---

[1] The whole of PartTwo and any other GBG manuals. [2] Brown, p.63. [3] pp.62,66. [4] pp. 62-65. [5] Depth of unmodified consciousness. [6] Flow, current, or thread of consciousness. [7] p.66 - the page margin.

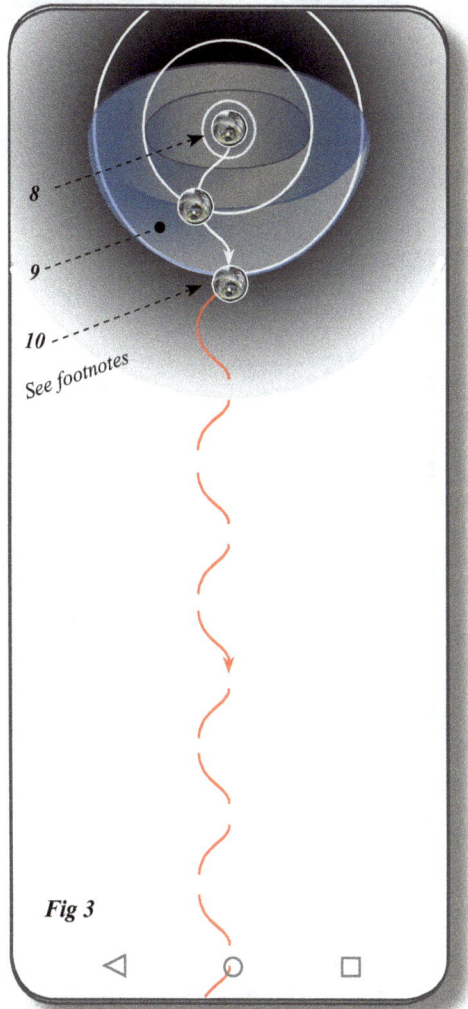

Fig 3

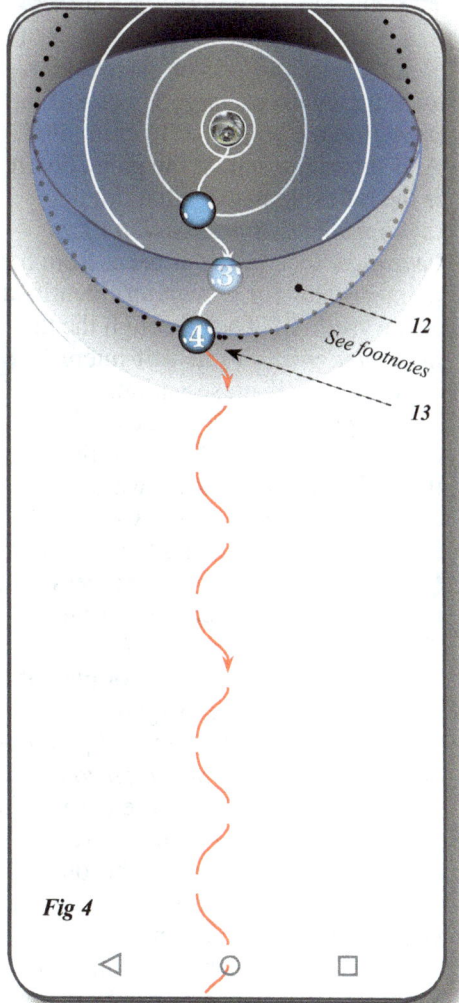

Fig 4

The "first distinction(s)" [11]

Every game begins spontaneously with **passive** *appearance* 🌀 of potentially the sign ① or the word for that appearance, the word ② for its object, and finally the sign or word ③ for its interpret<u>ant</u> or predisposed readiness of the interpreter ❹ (as yet not in mind) to actively apprehend the *"effect"* of the sign, where otherwise there is merely spontaneous arising appearance 🌀.

The apparent "I"

The game ordinarily proceeds only with the added appearance, position, predisposition, and participation of the "I," the interpreter sign ❹. The "I's" apprehension or interpretation of itself is then somehow coincident and predetermined by the interpret<u>ant</u> ③ making the "I" the **fourthness**[14] of the sign, the appearance, even prior to the "I" having apprehension of itself.

---

[8] First or cognitive <u>spheres</u> of consciousness. [9] Trichotomic appearance of cognitive <u>signs</u> of distinction. [10] pp.63. [11] The sphere(s) of mere appearance. [12] The viewpoint or the "I" in the game. [13] The observer in and of the game. [14] p.57.

T he turning point: *Fig 5* shows a trichotomy of spheres ● of Consciousness or placeholders awaiting conative *apprehension* of the *appearance* ①②③, not yet in mind. And superimposed on the game board is the reflexive path ↶ that mind, or the immediate **apprehension of appearance,** then takes, as seen, from the point-of-view (or view*point*) identified as the "self" ④, back through the then *thought-signs* ⋰ of its self-interest, comfort, or self-preservation.

Fig 6 shows the reflexive signs or *beads* of thought, having followed that reflexive path back toward self and now named from that viewpoint ④ in mind—completing the other half, ⑤⑥⑦, of the *arc*[1] of the process called thought, or now called *"metasphere: The flaw in the play of mind.*

Fig 7 shows a readout or play of successive metaspheres (games). Note that the *active* interpret<u>ant</u> *"disposition or readiness of the interpreter to respond to the sign,[2]"* or more clearly, the response or reaction to the *active* sign of the previous metasphere becomes ⑦ the passive *interpretant* ① of the next metasphere in-form-ation.

Each metasphere individually or a cluster of metaspheres can be read as a **sentence** or period (.) of thought and the *"characters"* in the *word-signs* transcribed as *the "script of the Game"* and all finally recorded and archived as the *"summary formula"* or *metaspheric perspective* on a topic. To this point the process can be described as the **ordinary round of play** —the usual outcome and *purpose* of mind or of the *Game.* Yet, according to the more esoteric manuals of the game, there are deeper levels of play that demand a degree of mastery.

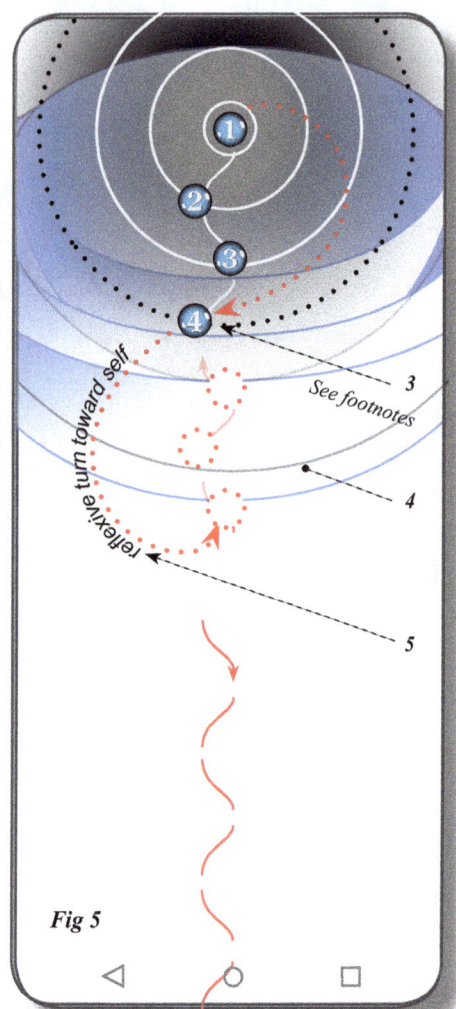

Fig 5

The turning point:

Thinking is a *reflexive event*—a *"turning"* ↶ or ↗ *"arc* [1]*"* in the *process* of mind. The manuals describe it as the **conative** apprehension of **cognitive** appearance, inclusive, not only of the evolutionarily conditioned *"reflex"* itself, but of all the predisposition ("bias") that "self" ④ has otherwise acquired, which determines the *script of the game* [6] readout from the *"glass bead"* (signs).

---

[1] Young, p.69. [2] Peirce, p.55. [3] The "self." [4] The active trichotomy of spheres of apprehension.
[5] Evolutionary purpose of mind. [6] Seen inside the bead, like the classic "magic 8-ball" [google it]..

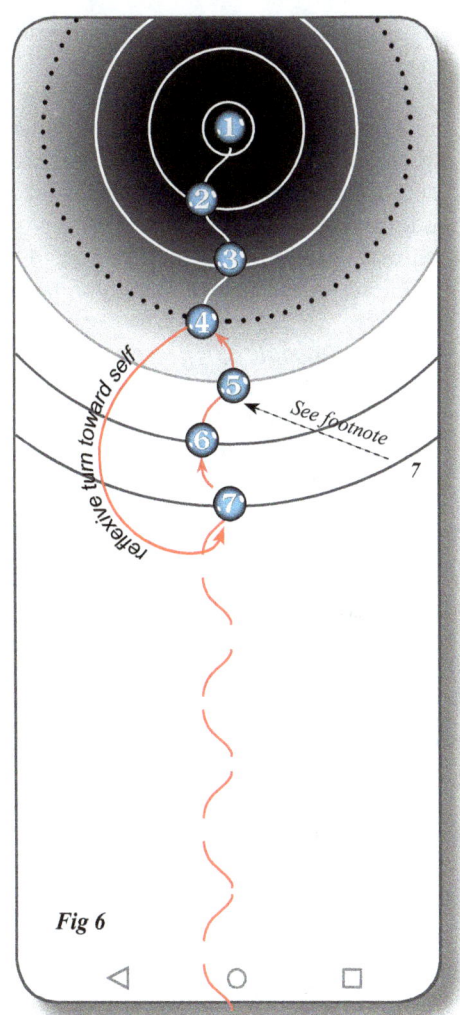

Fig 6

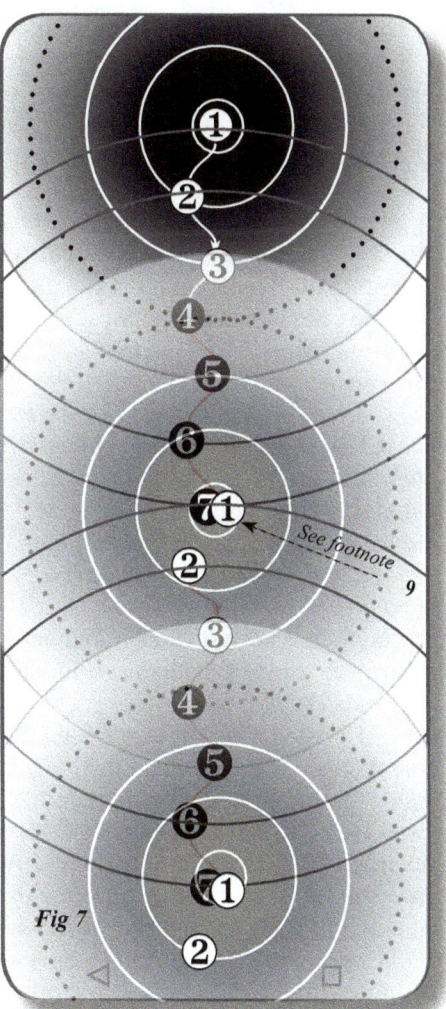

Fig 7

Apprehension of appearance:

When an *appearance* ①②③ comes to mind, the leading influence on its apprehension is Peirce's *"interpretant* [8] ③ or *"predisposed readiness"* of the *interpreter* ④ to respond with a reflexive apprehension ⑤⑥⑦. Such *"predisposition"* would seem to imply a *predetermined* result, which in today's quantum-speak, Peirce might have called the *"observer effect"* or similar quantum entanglement.

The ordinary play of mind:

Fig 6 (preceding screen) shows the stop action sequence of a single metasphere. And ordinarily, as represented here in *Fig 7,* thought goes on without hesitation, one metasphere and Game set after another, awake or in dreaming sleep. However there is a point at which biased or self-first thought can be *repurposed* with extraordinary or *"mastery"* play of *second thought.*

---

[7] The last sign of apprehension becomes the first sign of appearance, see fig 7. [8] Peirce, p.55.
[9] The first sign of appearance in the next sphere in any cluster of metaspheres.

In the esoteric Game manuals it is written that somehow one must get beyond, or transcend, the game to be a true *"master of the Game,"*—*"a personality that is cultivated enough to subordinate his own inspirations to the inviolable inner laws of the Game itself"*[1]—although such a personality, or person, will likely remain in the game for the sake of mentoring those *students* of mind still learning its *inviolable laws* and nuances.

"At various times the Game [has been] taken up and imitated by nearly all the scientific and scholarly disciplines. ...Each discipline that seized upon the Game created its own language of formulas, abbreviations, and possible combinations,"[2] which certainly has been demonstrated here. However, none of that is itself indicative of *"mastery play*[3]*."*

The reader can only presume that the words **"subordinate**[1]**"** and **"inspiration**[1]**"** translate from the German the way Hesse would have intended. However, given the importance of those two ideas in truly *"mastering"* the *Game*, it is worth some speculation as to what H.H. was really trying to say—speculation that might also apply to the other words in the phrase: *"personality," "cultivated,"* and *"enough."*[4] Surely these ideas account for the thousands of years of mystique given to the Game—for how would one *cultivate* such mastery aside from mentored play or by accident? Perhaps there is a clue in those Game manuals preceding the Castalian era—perhaps in the manual that you are reading now—a manual with an actual account of a mystic's feeling discovery of "surrender" into a nullstate and discerning the **nullpoint** in that state.

Figures 8 and 9 are the *feeling observation* of how the *discontinuous* "I" ① **phases in and out** rather than *pops* in and out of the Game (mind, or metasphere) allowing a pause or *gap* of unspecified duration between *appearance* and *apprehension* of *appearance*, before coalescing as "self" again. Masters of the Game call that underlying *gap* the *Nullpoint* ✥. In my own experience, I felt this *nullstate* as *"presence,"* and defined it as the surrendered state,[5] "subordinate to [my] own-self inspiration.[4]"

This *arising* and *fading* accounts for the **discontinuousness** of the "I." And interestingly, all that phasing occurs in the *"affectual*[6]*"* or median ○○○○ module of mind, which accounts for the second definition of *"affect:"* to give the *appearance of*, or *pretend*, which is to say the "I" does not arise as an *entity;* rather, it arises as a **"pretence or artificial process,"** — or mere **viewpoint.**

The *affectual* mode and that *pretence* were experientially realized in the author's entheogenic session:

"They [these others] were merely an apprehension of my own person-ality and could, should, and would vanish as mere thoughts— these were not entities."[7]

When the "I" ④ *phases out*, or is *surrendered*, I called it the "surrender event.[5]" When the ④ "I" *phases in*, the caption on the Game board[8] reads: *Having fallen off the razor's edge, "I" find my-self in the game.* Whereas, technically, the flow of consciousness ➚ has simply crossed over the ○○○○ median of metasphere from *cognitive* or merely witnessed spheres of appearance to the reflexive spheres of *apprehension* or *conative* mode of thinking.

---

[1] Hesse, GBG snippet p.46. [2] Quote from the GBG book. [3] Previous page. [4] Last sentence of 2nd column snippet p.82. [5] p.20. [6] p.59. [7] p.7. [8] p.83.

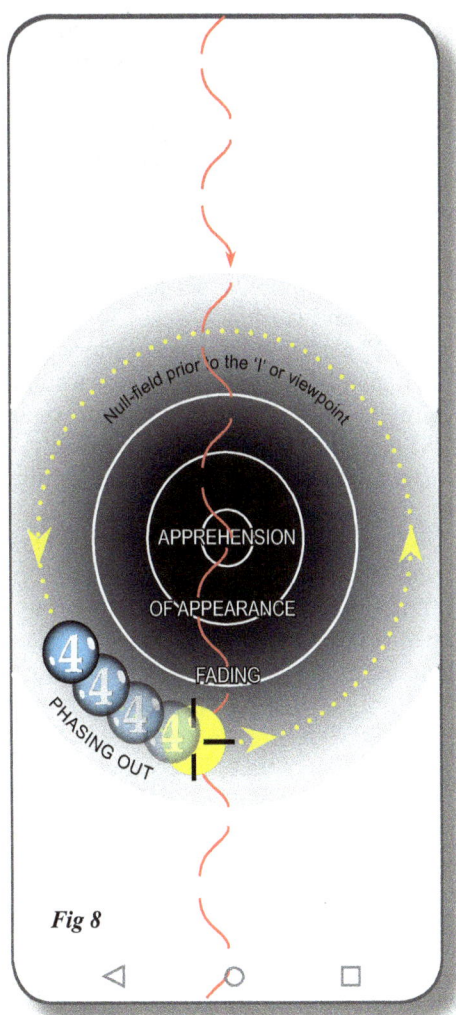

Fig 8

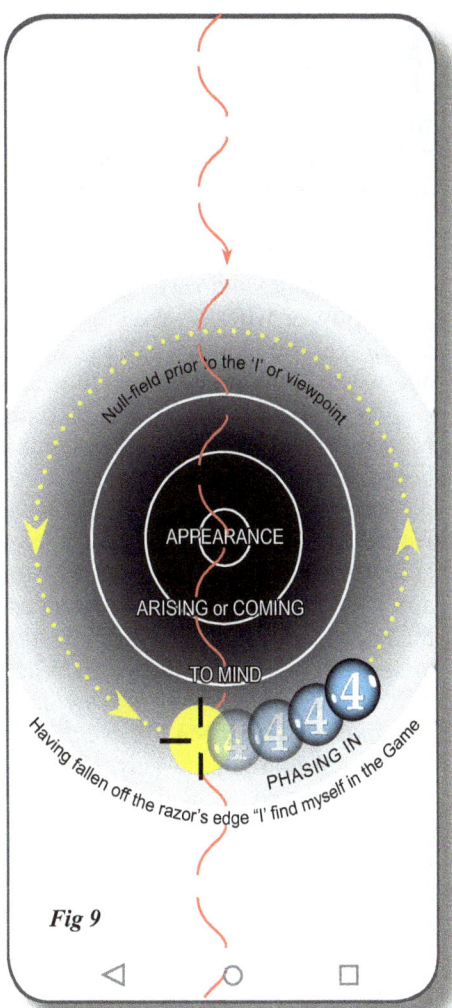

Fig 9

The discontinuous "I"

Phasing **in** rather than the phasing **out** of the ④ "I" is the more familiar, but it is the gap or nullpoint ✛ between *in* and *out* where mastery is acquired.

"Between stimulus and response there is a space. In that space is our power to choose our response. In our response lies our growth and freedom."
–Viktor E. Frankl, and attributed to Steven R. Covey.

The un-marked "gap"

Some refer to the "nullpoint" ✛ as *"the razor's edge,*[9]*"* for it cannot be tread long before all the evolutionary forces that give rise to the "I" or self come back into play. And since the ✛ priorly underlies the "I" or "viewpoint," both points cannot share the same space and time. And as antecedent to the experience of viewpoint,[2] the ✛ nullpoint cannot be experienced or observed by the ④ "I."

---

[9] Somerset Maugham p.77.

Here then, after the reader and author have together navigated "metasphere," each of us might well ask how do I *"subordinate"* the "I," or otherwise *surrender* one's self? Whereas it is only the "You," as in the *nullstate* or Consciousness itself,[1] that can do this. The writer, not very well, answers: there is no way, at least no *telling* of how or when or even if one will acquire that spontaneous mastery, nor if and when acquired, it will endure.

One might explain it like a *yoga (a yoke)*. The word *"yoga"* can mean both the *"event"* and the *"practice"(the how)* for acquiring the *event (the yoke)*. However, according to *masters of the Game,* such a dual definition serves only as a handicap: The *beginner* mistakes the *practice* for the yoga and the *student* mistakes the *event* for the yoga. Whereas, the true master assumes the yoke, or *no separation* between the *event* and the *practice,* from the very start.

So how do "you" do the yoga? The answer still stands: "I" cannot affect mind, for the "I" is mind. Thus, half the answer is to remember that "You" are not mind; the other half is to know who or what "You" are as consciousness —already surrendered prior to mind.

Understanding the "self," the "I" *person-ality* as no more than a *pretence* leaves one with a responsibility for the "self" but without "You" being bound by that evolutionarily acquired or conditioned, predisposed or biased *viewpoint*. This might be where "you" ask the *Game manuals'* infamous question: *"Who, or what, are 'you'?"* Ask your self "who" is this "one" that is bound? Is it not the "self," the "I"? Feelingly observe this in relation to the Game.

Are "**You**" not the "one" above or transcendent to the Game board, to the "territory[1]," to "self," to mind? Are "You" not the "one" *present* somewhere in the *"Null-field* **prior** *to the "I"'* or *viewpoint?*[2] Are You not Consciousness, the *Nullpoint* ✛ itself, — not the "I," not the "self?" Your answers open the deeper levels of play that demand *mastery.*

"I" certainly have no mastery of the game, but there are masters around. In my own story[3] my first master was *"Kundalini,"* who or which feelingly instructed body and mind in the trinity of ***presence-surrender-bliss.***

Decades later I came to sit with and be instructed by flesh and blood masters[4] of the Game through their bodily ***presence***, spoken and printed word, which evidently provided the understanding required *"to subordinate one's own inspiration"*[5] or *"to surrender one's own viewpoint"* into that place which is surrender itself—that prior and immediate transcendence made available to mind in every moment at the *Nullpoint* ✛ where and while the *script of the Game* is, as yet, unwritten.

Figures 10-14, of *"Game scripts"* are typical examples of the *apprehension* of *appearance* one might have while behind the wheel or as a passenger in a late afternoon traffic jam. **Put yourself in the driver's seat** and compare how the *Game* is played as a beginner,[6] a student,[7] and finally as a master.[8] Note the *"type of conation"* likely to arise at that point ● in which you have the **opportunity** to respond more or less *reflexively,* depending on the degree "the yoga," of the Game is perceived as a *practice,* or as a spontaneous and prior *event.*

---

[1] Graphic p.76.   [2] p.65.   [3] PartOne p.28.   [4] See tribute, p.109.   [5] Hesse, p.82.   [6] p.91.   [7] p.92.   [8] pg 93.

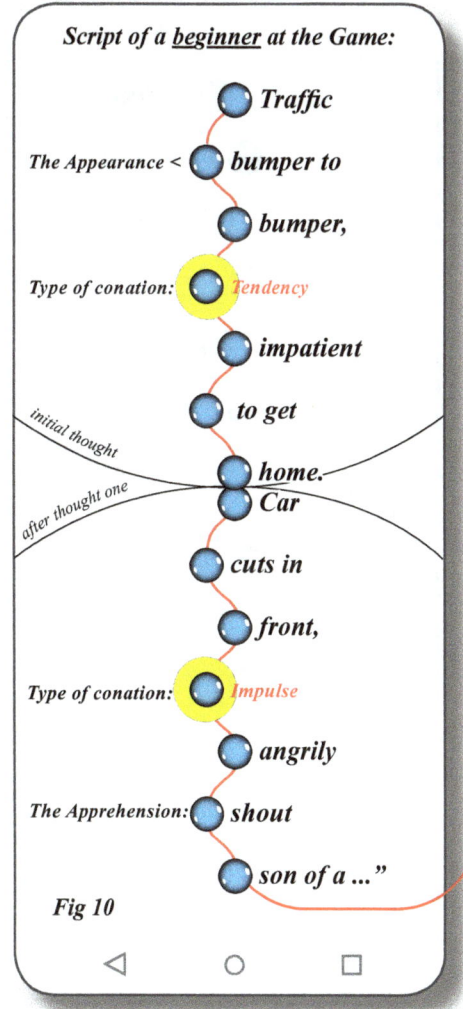

Fig 10

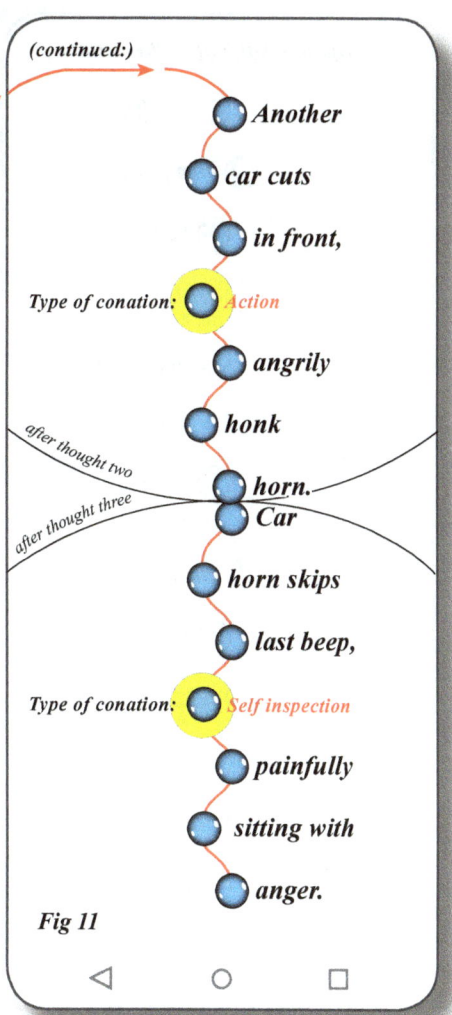

Fig 11

The initial thoughts

Initial or first thoughts are most often automatic, **reflexively** arising by tendency, impulse, or mental or bodily action, which may include vocalization, gesture, or even physical behavior, and all without afterthought. Mastery begins to come into play when, by self-inspection, pause or by some means or practice, the player sees how the first course of thought is inherently flawed with "self".

The afterthoughts

Mastering game-play is about second thought opening *up* to the background flow of *undifferentiated* ⊙ consciousness while intermittently actively involved in *differentiated* ◯ mind and eventually allowing consciousness (or the avataric "You") to *descend*, ▽ while letting mind *ascend*, △ leveling the playing field, so to speak, accessing information otherwise inaccessible.

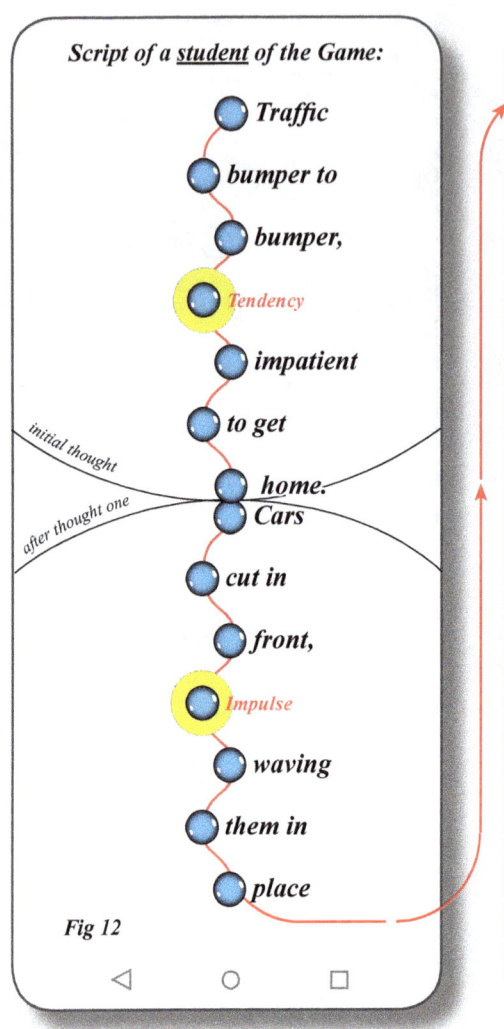
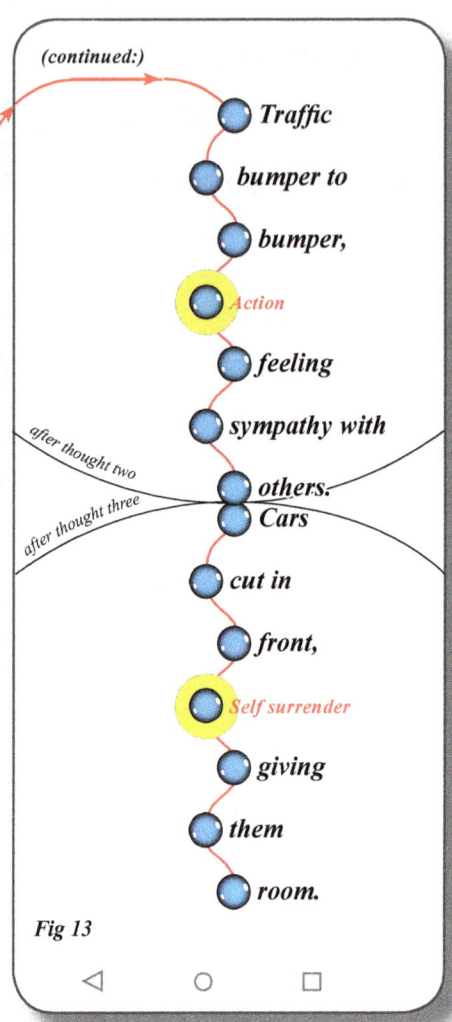

Fig 12

Fig 13

"Script of the Game"

Not surprisingly, the etymology of the word "surrender" holds the most relevant meaning in its prefix "**sur-**" *(super, or transcendent)* and in the reflexive sense "to give oneself *up*" in the *rendering* or *apprehension* of appearance, which in practice, *subordinates* one's "self" or *pretentious "I"* viewpoint — something only possible if "You" *(as nullpoint)* are presently, or already, surrender itself.

"The Summary Formula"

Allow as many *afterthoughts* as necessary to determine *"the validity of the initial thought,"*[1] —that most *"subordinate of our own inspirations,"*[2] that most *"sur-rendered viewpoint."* Yet, there will be no final or completely *unbiased* outcome. For that would require no *distinction,* no viewpoint, no thought, thus no mind. Therefore, there is no choice but to **repurpose mind.**

---

[1] PartTwo J. H. Beck, p.58. [2] Hesse GBG excerpt, p.82.

I suppose at this point, our standing in the *Game* is somewhere between a beginner and student practice, so we can only guess what *"masterful play"* looks like[1]. But if we were that *"...cultivated enough to [surrender] [our] own inspirations to the inviolable inner laws of the Game itself,"* then we would know those *"inner laws"* and that the *First Law* is that the *"game itself,"* thus *mind itself, certainly "self" itself,* results from *"acquisition of language*[2] which set the Game in motion to begin with. We would know the *Second Law,* the *nullpoint* or tacit *gap* where surrender priorily resides, awaiting the *turn* toward it rather than toward *"self."* That "giving "self" up, like sleep, is nothing the "self" can command of it"self," but only *allow* and constantly *prepare* for. We would know the *Third Law,* the *Endgame* or surrender of language, words, thought, or self, which *allows* for the *tacit,* inexplicable *silent-hearing* and *real-seeing* of *what is* always just prior to what the *reflexive* "self," with its biased *point of view,* has to say.

And if you recall the *Preface,*[3] now is the time for *testing* this phenomenological discovery. *Simply close the book, let the headgear fall away, and observe metasphere and metaspheric perspective from "Your" now unbound liberated position. Perhaps you are already leaning toward repurposing mind, from a less confined, more transcendent position, or seat of realization.* ▲

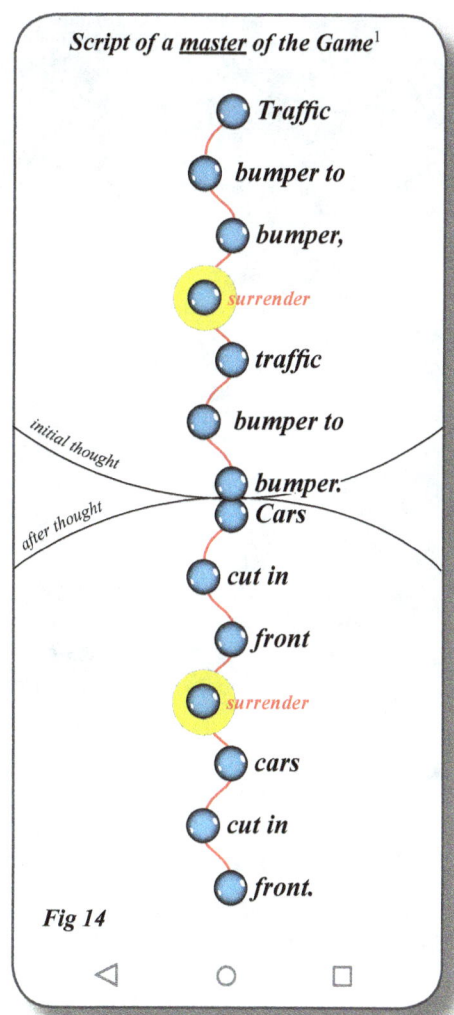

Script of a <u>master</u> of the Game[1]

Fig 14

The Endgame

Some might say that mastery of the *Game* is itself *self-serving*. Well, of course it is. That understanding is the point, a point undone by seeing the *self* as what you do, not what You are—that is the *endgame*.

The game rules advise one not merely to be mentored by one of the many masters of mind, but to locate a true Master of Consciousness, one not in the Game.

---

[1] Game screen, this page. [2] Lowe, PartTwo, p.45. [3] Preface p.vii.

Hesse's vision of Castalia:

To follow this next section, it is not necessary to be all that familiar with Hermann Hesse's book *Magister Ludi*, nor with Leary's *The Politics of Ecstasy*. However, a QR link to each book is provided below.

In *The Politics of Ecstasy,* Leary had much to say about Hesse's vision of Castalia. For Tim, as well as Richard, and Ralph, Castalia became a conscious element in their own "set," and as good a "setting" and vision for their cultural experiment at Millbrook.

Whereas Tim may have been the revolutionary, putting all his hopes in brain scientism, Hesse, on the other hand, had put his bet on a philosophy of mind. Both bets lost in the end.

The "League" is a running theme in Hesse's writings which refers to outliers such as you and me, and is particularly elaborated in his 1932 book *Journey to the East.*

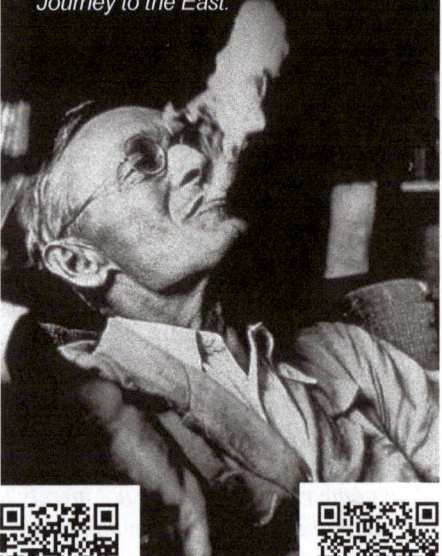

Hermann Karl Hesse, 1877-1962

"The Last Glass Bead Game Player"

Poem from Joseph Knecht's Posthumous Writings, told in Hermann Hesse's 1943 book Magister Ludi,

"The color beads, his playthings, in his hand,

He sits head bent; around him lies a land

Laid waste by war and ravaged by disease.

Growing on rubble, ivy hums with bees;

A weary peace with muted psalmody

Sounds in a world of aged tranquility.

The old man tallies up his colored beads:

He fits a blue one here, a white one there,

Makes sure a large one, or a small, precedes,

And shapes his Game ring with devoted care.

Time was he had won greatness in the Game,

Had mastered many tongues and many arts,

Had known the world, traveled in foreign parts

— From pole to pole, no limits to his fame.

Around him pupils, colleagues always pressed.

Now he is old, worn-out; his life is lees.

Disciples come no longer to be blessed,

Nor masters to invite an argument.

All, all are gone, and the temples, libraries,

And schools of Castalia are no more. At rest

Amid the ruins, the glass beads in his hand,

Those hieroglyphics once so significant

That now are only colored bits of glass,

He lets them roll until their force is spent

And silently they vanish in the sand."

Tribute

To the League of Students & Masters of the Game

In particular: Hermann Hesse, Timothy Leary, and including
Ram Dass, Ralph Metzner, Jakob Böhme, René Daumal, Buckminster Fuller,
Peter Mark Roget, Charles S. Peirce, and Avatar Adi Da Samraj

Since I have already liberally appropriated Hesse's most enlightening fictional theme, the *Glass Bead Game,* my reader might initially object to my also using his fictional theme: the "*League of Eastern Wayfarers,*[1] in this, my non-fiction treatise. Yet, I am proud to join Tim Leary in such appropriating behavior. Leary was so sympathetic with Hesse's vision of *Castalia* that he and his cohorts Alpert and Metzner formed the *Castalia Foundation* — replacing the previous front organization IFIF, *International Federation for Internal Freedom,* which had funded the early issues of *The Psychedelic Review* and had the likes of Huston Smith, Julian Huxley, and Alan Watts on the editorial advisory board. Thus the vision of Hesse's pedagogic community of *Castalia* became the "set" and "setting" of Leary's Millbrook.

Huston Smith was one of many willing to lend their prominence to Leary's mission. Smith would say: "*The goal of spiritual life is not altered states, but altered traits*"— a statement similar to Watts' admonition to "do the *work.*" The idea of a *"game"* being used as a practice in that effort is interesting in light of this excerpt from IFIF's mission statement:

> *"The human cortex is the same—east and west. What differs are the cultural games. Games, being artifacts, can be changed. New games spontaneously and naturally arise."* – (Excerpt from IFIF charter)

Only a few of the thousands of visitors to Millbrook and the hundreds of its residents, over the years, were even aware of Tim's vision of Castalia, which is perhaps why the hermitage became better known as Millbrook, rather than its founding name "Castalia Foundation." Even for Tim, the vision had long since vanished by the time Millbrook closed in 1968. The "*wayfarers,* the founders, likely endured the closing with: "*A weary peace with muted psalmody. Sounds in a world of aged tranquility.*"[2]

---

[1] Hesse, *Journey to the East,* 1932.   [2] See facing page.

A respectable number of people were reading Hesse in the 1960's, and I imagine it was Metzner, since he was born in Hesse's hometown of Berlin, Germany, who likely introduced Leary and Alpert to this great author. We do know that Metzner, as editor of the *Psychedelic Review,* coauthored with Leary an essay *The Poet of the Inner Journey*—a direct tribute to Hesse and to Leary's belief that Hesse most likely had imbibed psychedelics. The essay first appeared in the *Review* and later in Leary's book *The Politics of Ecstasy,* 1968.

"FROM POLE TO POLE, NO LIMITS TO HIS FAME"[1]

In the essay, Leary speaks specifically to three[2] of Hesse's books, and mainly to the parallels between Hesse's character Knecht or *Magister Ludi* and Leary's own life and mission. The lead voice in the essay is Metzner, providing analysis and readings along with a narration of Hesse's life and real-life acquaintances that may have figured as characters in his books. The second voice in the essay is Leary speaking to Metzner's research and analysis, as well as quoting Hesse directly. Hesse's is the third voice.

Leary's suspicion that Hesse took a psychedelic comes out of the fact that his real-life travels to the East, to Sri Lanka, Indonesia, Sumatra, Borneo, and Burma, would have provided a familiarity with psychoactive drugs.

Hesse's book *Steppenwolf (1927)* was certainly the smoking gun (or pipe) for Leary's belief that H.H. had at some time or other in real life experienced psychedelic states of consciousness. And given the narrative in *Steppenwolf* with *Harry's* friend *Pablo* (a dope fiend and traveling jazz player), the likelihood is that there was also a pipe, or two, of hashish involved.

Leary's voice (in reference to a scene in Hesse's Steppenwolf):

> *"It seems clear that Hesse is describing a psychedelic experience, a drug-induced loss of self, a journey in the inner world. Each door in the 'Magic Theatre' has a sign on it, indicating the endless possibilities of the experience."* — Leary, The Politics of Ecstasy (Chapter: Poet of the Interior Journey)

Leary's voice (in reference to post-session integration):

> *"So Harry Haller, the Steppenwolf, had his psychedelic session,*

---

[1] Hesse, Last GBG Player, p.94.   [2] *Siddhartha, Steppenwolf, and Magister Ludi.*

discovered instead of one reality, infinite realities within the brain...

He is admitted into the select group of those who have passed through the verbal curtain into other modes of consciousness. He has joined the elite brotherhood... And then what? Where do you go from there? How can the holy sense of unity and revelation be maintained? Does one sink back into the somnambulant world of rote passion, automated action, egocentricity?" —Leary, The Politics of Ecstasy (Poet of the Interior Journey) excerpt from p.183

Hesse's voice (likewise, in reference to post-session integration):

"That almost all of us and also I, even I should again lose myself in the soundless deserts of mapped out reality, just like officials and shop assistants who, after a party or a Sunday outing, adapt themselves again to everyday business life!" — H.H. Journey to The East

Leary's voice:

"These are issues faced by everyone who has passed into a deep, transego experience. How can we preserve the freshness, illuminate each second of subsequent life? How can we maintain the ecstatic oneness with others?" — Leary, The Politics of Ecstasy (Poet of the Interior Journey) excerpt from p.83

Author's (my) voice:

For Leary and perhaps anyone of us, it's not only about maintaining the *"ecstatic oneness with others"* but how to maintain common courtesies and relationships with "others," and *"adapt(ing)... to everyday business life!"*

Early on, at Millbrook, Leary and fellow Castalian *Metzner* had become uneasy about the direction the Castalian School had taken, and for some unexplained reason (abruptly) asked fellow Castalian Alpert to leave Millbrook, or rather *"not come back"* to Millbrook.

Alpert, Leary's most experienced game partner did leave and did not come back to Millbrook. He went to India, and returned from his journey to the East renamed by the guru he met there, who gave him the devotee name "Ram Dass," servant of God. Ram Dass went on to *Remind* us to *Be here Now*.

Leary's voice (a message to the psychedelic culture at large):

> *"Groups which attempt to apply psychedelic experiences to social living will find in the story of Castalia all the features and problems which such attempts inevitably encounter: the need for a new language or set of symbols... the central importance of maintaining direct contact with the regenerative forces of the life process through meditation... the crucial and essentially insoluble problem of the relation of the mystic community to the world at large. Can the order remain an educative, spiritual force in the society, or must it degenerate through isolation and inattention to a detached, alienated group of idealists?*
>
> *Every major and minor social renaissance has had to face this problem. Hesse's answer is clear: the last part of the book consists of three tales, allegedly written by Knecht, describing his life in different incarnations. In each one the hero devotes himself wholeheartedly to the service and pursuit of an idealist, spiritual goal, only to recognize at the end that he has become the slave of his own delusions."*
>
> — Leary, The Politics of Ecstasy (Poet of the Interior Journey) excerpt from p.187

These are obvious cautions to future students and masters of the *Game*, under that same fateful *delusion*. Certainly Leary was quite aware that his social experiment was a risk to his own freedom, and to the mystic community at large. Hopefully the current *Psychedelic Renaissance* will fare much better.

It might also be obvious that Leary's experiment suffered the *"...need for a new language or set of symbols,"* the one way the *"mystic community can remain an educative, spiritual force in the society."*

Leary's voice in regard to *Magister Ludi / The Glass Bead Game:*

> *"Most readers miss the message of Hesse. Entranced by the pretty dance of plot and theme, they overlook the seed message ... the electrical message, the code..."* — The Politics of Ecstasy, excerpt p.178

The narrator in Hesse's *The Glass Bead Game* tells the reader right up front: *"No such thing as a textbook on the game will ever be written."* If the unwritten intention is for the reader to figure out the code him or herself, then Hesse's goal was certainly fulfilled. And even if the message is that no one can figure out the code or mechanisms by which mind works, they need only review the limning of discoveries in this book.

In Leary's book *Flashbacks (1983)*, he tells of an event on his own tour of India, not as profound as to earn a new name, like Ram Dass, but very telling of Leary's own search for wisdom and/or guru: One day, he obeyed a strong intuition to get to the forested bank of the river Ganges, across from the pilgrim throng on the other shore in the city of Banãras. He hired a ferryman and, upon stepping off onto the forested bank, unexpectedly received fleeting darshan (sighting) of a barely clothed avadhoot (yogi ascetic). Leary was immediately inspired to chase after the running figure, perhaps a reflection of himself in some other life. But the ferryman, reluctant to wait, threatened to leave without Leary aboard. Leary, equally reluctant, got back in the boat. And likely, for the rest of his life, pondered the meaning of that extraordinary event.

Both Leary and Hesse put their all into their writings. Hesse's experiences shaped his themes; his themes in turn shaped his journey. His early apprenticing in bookshops put him in easy proximity to the cream of human understanding of the game, including his first interests: the German Romantics, Buddhism, and Theosophy. His brief formal study in seminary gave him a slight Christian bent, but otherwise his writings opened to all wisdom traditions.

Leary's literary legacy, *The Politics of Ecstasy* and his other works, are safely archived in New York City's Public Library. Which is not to diminish his two colleagues' literary legacy: Ram Dass' book *Remember: Be Here Now*, and Metzner's *Maps of Consciousness*. Theirs was, and still is, a covert message, typical of Eastern *Yogic* and both East & West *Shamanic* tradition. While Leary's message was dangerously overt, wide open to social, political, and even scientific criticism, misunderstanding, and false interpretation.

Both Hesse and Leary became overnight controversial figures due to their *"attempt... to apply love to matters political..."* For H.H., the matter was his homeland's wars on Europe, now known as the World Wars. For Leary, it was a similar circumstance: a frightened and arrogant government, itself in the midst of a war in the far East, and all too anxious to start and sustain a homeland war over the re-discovered "united states" of consciousness.

---

[1] The Last GBG Player, p.94.

"THE OLD MAN TALLIES UP HIS COLORED BEADS" [1]

I could stop at this point, take the beads that I have already strung on my *"game ring,"* skip the requisite meditation, and thus bring this Tribute to a speedy end without tribute to some of the other members of the League.

But then I would not have fully answered the extent to which I myself am sympathetic to Hesse's most hidden message and code, which has more relevance today, in light of the psychedelic renaissance, global crises, and to the treatise of the book you have in hand.

> *"It can be communicated, certainly, as I have communicated it to you just now. But it cannot be transmitted. I can make you understand my associations, but I cannot so affect a single one of you that my private association will become a valid symbol for you in your turn [of mind]..."* — H.H. excerpt from The Glass Bead Game

Leary's thorough gleaning of the *code* in *The Glass Bead Game,* which he added to his *The Politics of Ecstasy,* speaks to the inevitable political, cultural, and social difficulty that arise when there is any attempt to bottle a vision—the vision simply vanishes.

Leary's voice in summing up his essay:

> *"Castalia is essentially the League, frozen into a social institution."* —Leary, Politics of Ecstasy, excerpt from p.191

The *"League of Eastern Wayfarers,"* or a group of similar sort is a consistent theme in Hesse's later[2] works, specifically in his novel *Journey to the East (1927)*—something between an exotic travelog and search for wisdom, both East and West. The lead character and narrator *(H.H. himself)* tells of having mistakenly become disillusioned with the leadership of the *League.*

With that disillusion in mind, H.H. had deserted the League ten years earlier. But later he labors to tell the story of the *League,* and in the process discovers that a hidden agenda of the *League's* archivists, in addition to collecting the *"treasure trove"* of ancient texts and sacred art from the *Journey,* had surreptitiously been to record each *Wayfarer's* own experience on the journey, including the experience of the narrator H.H.

---

[1] Hesse, Last GBG Player, p.94. [2] Three Books: *Siddhartha, Steppenwolf, and Magister Ludi.*

H.H. recalls that the leaders called it a journey toward *"the place of light,"* a trek both forward and backward in time through many strange domains with allegorical names. My own book, this book, likewise has recorded and archived the explorations of a group of outliers who deserve tribute for the enlightened trove of their writings and discoveries.

Aside from Leary's assertion that the *League* are the elite brotherhood (and sisterhood) of only *"... those who have passed through the verbal curtain into other modes of consciousness,"* Hesse may have simply created a metaphor referring to the good company he kept in real-life, with friends, philosophers, mystics, and intellectuals, including the virtual community of authors and pundits in the varied books he and those others were reading—i.e. the testaments of mystic masters, the Vedas, Upanishads, and the assorted Gitas.

As for the *League's Journey to the East,* Hesse gives this description:

"...our group had set off on its travels; soon we encountered other groups, and the feeling of unity and a common goal gave us increasing happiness. ... The expedition did not, in fact, proceed in any fixed order with participants moving in the same direction ...On the contrary, numerous groups were simultaneously on the way, each following their own leaders and their own stars, each one always ready to merge into a greater unit and belong to it for a time, but always no less ready to move on again separately. Some went on their way quite alone."[3]

In the last pages of *Journey to the East,* H.H. says, *"I in my simplicity, I wanted to write the story of the league, I, who could not decipher or understand one-thousandth part of those millions of scripts, books, pictures and reference in the archives!"*—this in remark to his being tried and acquitted of *"deserting"* the *League* and now given full access to the League *"archives."*

Although the *League* and its *archives* are not directly referred to in Hesse's 25th century story of *Magister Ludi, Castalia,* and the *Glass Bead Game,* one might surmise that after two World Wars, and likelihood of a third, the *League* would have found it imperative to secure its archive in a safe place. That place might have been that *"mountainous country*[3]*"* where the pedagogic community, to be called *Castalia,* would be founded. Where for the next 300 years, stragglers and descendants

---

[3] Hesse's *Magister Ludi - Glass Bead Game.*

from the *League* would have carefully unpacked those treasures of spiritual and intellectual understanding, and with technological advances, cloned the archive in a way for all future League members to easily access and research for their Games.

I imagine the original archive as well worn books, loose textual and music documents, audio & visual recordings, facsimile artworks—all imbedded in the *Glass Beads,* and made transparent to the insight of the *Game* players.

Embellishing Hesse's fictional narrative in this, my nonfiction narrative has had its playful side demonstrated in *PartThree*—using a *game* as the technology of last resort, since world governments have refused to fund remedial technology in the immediate time-frame necessary, or to halt operation of those technologies underlying and sustaining the global climate crisis.

And in this *Tribute* I hope to have countered any mistaken notion that Leary's revolutionary ideas were dangerous, whereas, in fact, Leary's cultural mind-hacking proved fifty years ago what neuro or brain-hacking is now calling the existence of a *"Default Mode Neuro)network"*—that script or voice, seemingly in your head, that I call "metaspheric perspective," the I, or self, or simply the structural self-pointing-logic I call "metasphere" or mind.

And perhaps more importantly, I hope all this raised the question of how the *"mystic community can remain an educative, spiritual force in society*[1]*"* at this critical time and in this peril to civilization.

Lastly, with all the billions of billions of billions of *Games* scripts generated every moment by the billions of beings on the planet, it is easy to imagine, at this rate, the *Game* is likely to be played indefinitely, yet mastered by few. What is not easy to imagine is how many of that "few" it will take to do that *conscious* game play of repurposing the otherwise unconscious self-first purposed mind to get through the crises and obligate themselves to rebuild civilization on the other side?

> **Reader be aware:** A recent online search for "Castalia Foundation" reveals that now, 60 years later, that name has apparently been "... co-opted to promote conspiracy theories..." –Source: Psymposia.com, Russel Hausfeld, Feb 2, 2021. A fair reading of Hausfeld's in depth article, along with a browsing of examples of those conspiracies published by an outfit calling itself Castalia Foundation, would seem to bear no resemblance to Hesse's nor Leary's vision, which most anyone reading the tribute above, would agree.

[1] p.98.

Tribute to my friend C. Michael Smith's scholarly review:

In this, Michael's kind review of the earlier Review Copy of this work, I took to heart his critique and hopefully improved the continuity of the argument. But, even as his remarks stand they impart my original intent that one read between the lines, feeling the mystery, as well as following the logic of the lines themselves.

"In this book we have a rigorous philosophic and phenomenological reflection of the nature of mind, its processes and limit structures, always making distinctions and separations... This is an unusual book and not an easy read from the point of view of getting a quick fix of information... One reason seems to be the author's intent to put you not through a standard text with well outlined linear argument, but to put you through a real philosophical engagement, even something like yogic practices whereby you can examine for yourself the author's points.

I approached the book in the predictable manner of a scholar[1], but was quickly stymied. I fanned through the pages, as the author predicted, perhaps even planned, and then turned to the beginning, and then began jumping around, looking for clues—I felt like a detective following-up on clues—tracking down a mystery...

This book, finally, leaves you with a clear sense of mystery. The mind indeed abhors unknowing, and the author makes this point, over time, in a massive spherical, and perhaps quasi-fractal way, subverting efforts to control the mystery of existence.

...One of my favorite snippets of info had to do with... Jung's position regarding kundalini, which I appreciated, as a Jungian scholar,[2] but it was his description of surrender in the kundalini process that I found highly resonant with hundreds of people I have worked with on four continents undergoing spiritual emergence. I work in a holotropic way, in a system I call sacred breath work. Spontaneous kriyas arise, and kundalini, where it has arisen can self-resolve when there is a kind of surrender the author so precisely described. He writes:

"The yoga one does is not The Yoga. The yoga one does is to release the pain of resistance to the Yoga that is already done."

...I have long observed from my own client work that the yogic asanas form spontaneously, and rishis have simply catalogued and taught them. The author insightfully points to a surrendering in which the body itself begins to guide the mind.

These are the impressions, and distinctions that come to my mind, as I reflect on the rich and diverse menu of this book."

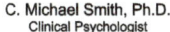

C. Michael Smith, Ph.D.
Clinical Psychologist

www.crowsnestshamanism.com

---

[1] See Biblio.: *Psycho-therapy and The Sacred*.   [2] *Jung and Shamanism in Dialog*

Tribute to Jakob Böhme's "Philofophic Globe" 1620 AD"

The facsimile page below describes one of the remarkable metagraphs that emerged out of The European Renaissance as typography and engraving allowed metagraphy to illuminate the page. This page is by the Christian mystic Jakob Böhme, *1575-1624*.

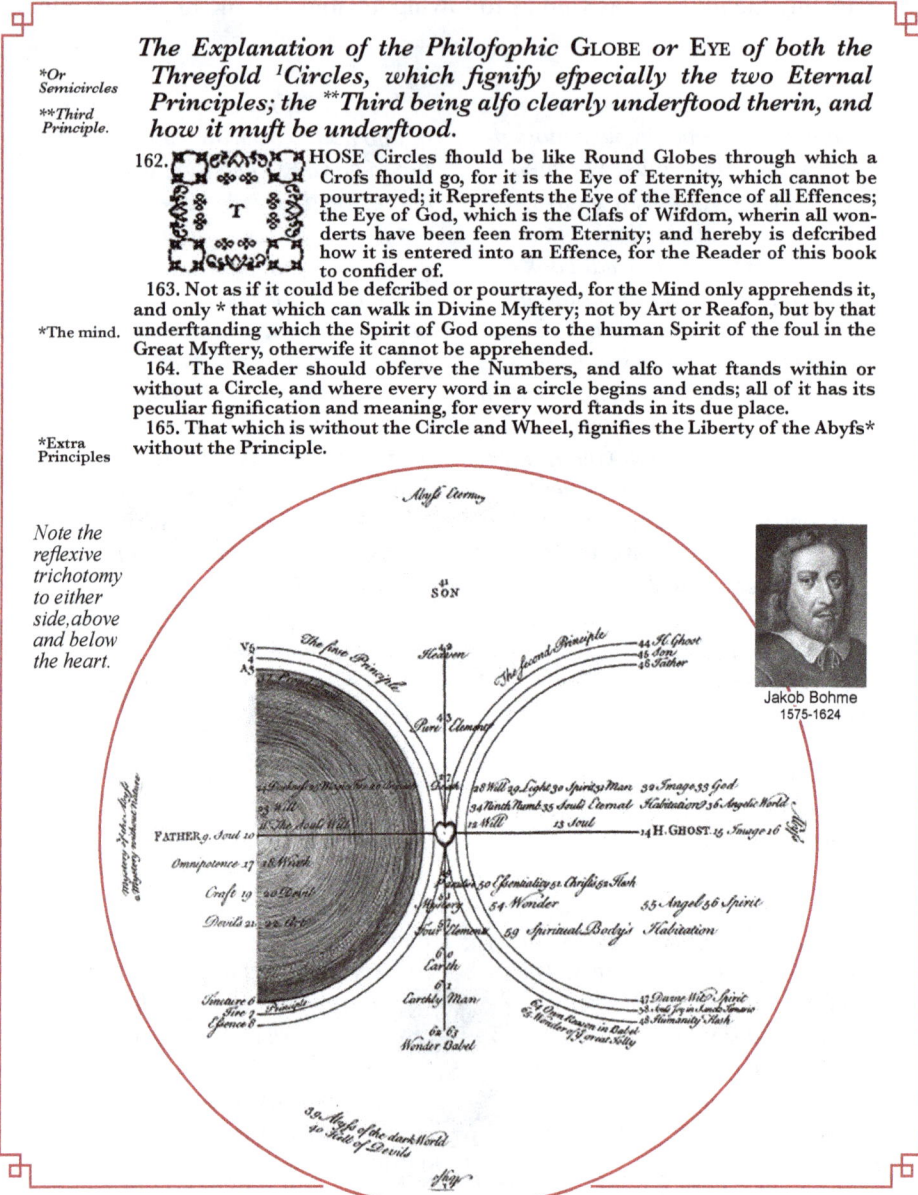

The Explanation of the Philofophic GLOBE *or* EYE *of both the Threefold ¹Circles, which fignify efpecially the two Eternal Principles; the **Third being alfo clearly underftood therin, and how it muft be underftood.*

*Or Semicircles
**Third Principle.

162. THOSE Circles fhould be like Round Globes through which a Crofs fhould go, for it is the Eye of Eternity, which cannot be pourtrayed; it Reprefents the Eye of the Effence of all Effences; the Eye of God, which is the Clafs of Wifdom, wherin all wonders have been feen from Eternity; and hereby is defcribed how it is entered into an Effence, for the Reader of this book to confider of.

163. Not as if it could be defcribed or pourtrayed, for the Mind only apprehends it, and only * that which can walk in Divine Myftery; not by Art or Reafon, but by that underftanding which the Spirit of God opens to the human Spirit of the foul in the Great Myftery, otherwife it cannot be apprehended.

*The mind.

164. The Reader should obferve the Numbers, and alfo what ftands within or without a Circle, and where every word in a circle begins and ends; all of it has its peculiar fignification and meaning, for every word ftands in its due place.

165. That which is without the Circle and Wheel, fignifies the Liberty of the Abyfs* without the Principle.

*Extra Principles

Note the reflexive trichotomy to either side, above and below the heart.

Jakob Bohme 1575-1624

Philofophic [sphere] or the *"Wonder Eye of Eternity"*
Jakob Böhme's 1620 drawing translated from the German for William Law, engraved by D. A. Freher 1764

1 of 4 serial volumes 1765 to 1781 of William Law. Note: Globe can mean "Sphere" and "Eye," the "I."

Tribute to Buckminster Fuller's Minimum Universe and to the mystic René Daumal's Surreal Universe:

*Fuller says: "A system is the simplest physical or metaphysical experience we humans can have. A system must always have insideness and outsideness... "In synergetic geometry we are able to consider the geometry of thought systems... Recognition of a system begins with the initial discovery of either **self** or **otherness**... [such] A system divides all Universe, convergently and divergently **separating** all the outwardness from all the inwardness and from the system itself, which does the dividing."*[1]

"...I have found the tetrahedron to be the minimum structural system Universe.[2] ...In time, the existence will be acknowledged of both the special-case physical, systematically considered Universe and the generalized metaphysical, comprehensive **tetrahedron Universe**.[3]... the metaphysical involves that which can be experienced but is independent of size, and is weightless and energyless, i.e. qualitative rather than quantitative ...The other at-minimum twoness of unity is the observer and observed, and their union is the realization of life—in pure principle.[5]"

*Also see Bibliography: **Synergetics** 1975 Explorations in the Geometry of Thinking, ¶ 483.00*

"In the beginning the **sphere** and **tetrahedron** were united in a single inconceivable form: concentration and expansion mysteriously fused in a single will, which willed only its own being. There came a separation but the unique remains unique. The sphere became primordial man, who wishing to realize **separately** all of his desires, scattered himself into all the animal species and men of today. The tetrahedron became..." Mount Analogue (pg 83)

See Bibliography: Rene Daumal (1986) **Mount Analogue** *(Published posthumously) Shambhala Gold Books*

Buckminster Fuller's vision is more of the physical variety, whereas, I am sure, Daumal is thinking metaphysically.

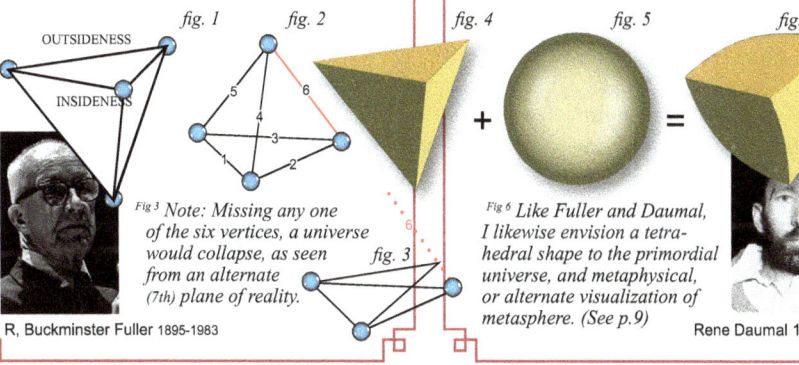

fig. 1   fig. 2   fig. 4   fig. 5   fig. 6

OUTSIDENESS
INSIDENESS

Fig 3 Note: Missing any one of the six vertices, a universe would collapse, as seen fig. 3 from an alternate (7th) plane of reality.

Fig 6 Like Fuller and Daumal, I likewise envision a tetrahedral shape to the primordial universe, and metaphysical, or alternate visualization of metasphere. (See p.9)

R, Buckminster Fuller 1895-1983   Rene Daumal 1908-1944

[1] See Biblio.: 1992: *Cosmography, Aposthumous scenario for the future of humanity. Edited by Adjuvant Kiyoshi Kuromyiyap,* pp124-125. [2]Ibid, p.41. [3]Ibid p.47. [4]Ibid, p.48. [5]Ibid, p.49.

Roget's categorization versus Dewey's classification:

Classification vs. *categorization* of ideas (words) would seem to be an intuitive analogue to the polar symmetry of the model of mind (metasphere) and metaspheric perspective offered in this book. So, let's closely examine these *opposing* poles.

Regrettably, Dewey's outlook was the the <u>divergence</u> of ideas:

Ordinarily, we do not think there is much difference between **categorization** and **classification**. Yet that difference has contributed to a kind of *information pollution*. In metaspheric perspective the **cognitive** pole can be compared to categorization and the **conative** pole to classification (or arbitrary and bias based thought). If you are asking how classification is **biased**, consider this definition of a classification process.

> "Classification as process involves the orderly and systematic assignment of each entity to one and only one class within a system of mutually exclusive and non-overlapping classes. ...The scheme itself is **artificial and arbitrary**: artificial because it is a tool created for the express purpose of establishing a meaningful organization; and arbitrary because the criteria used to define classes in the scheme reflect a single perspective of the domain to the exclusion of all other perspectives. Classification is the term used to refer to three distinct but related concepts: a system of classes, ordered according to a predetermined set of principles and used to organize a set of entities; a group or class in a classification system ..."
> – Elin K. Jacob, Indiana University

Regrettably the dominant system of classification of information is the Dewey Decimal System, established in 1876. Helpful to libraries but as artificial & arbitrary a view of reality as ever designed.

Melvil Louis Dewey
1851-1931

Dewey's likely anthropocentric view is countered by a more generous view offered by a Dewey advocate:

> "Dewey began with man and his relation to himself and the world **(100 Philosophy)**, then man in relation to the transcendent **(200 Religion)** and to man in relation to others **(300 Social Science)** and how relation is understood **(400 Language)**; and then in relation to reality, **(500 Science)** and in relation to the world **(600 Technology)**; then in relation to beauty and form **(700 Arts)** and abstractly in relation to **(800 Literature)**; then in relation to all that, in time and place **(900 History & Geography)**."
> —gettingintoholywater.com/page/3/

Notice how all of these are man-made distinctions, man in relation to him*self*, to his achievements. To see Dewey's own bias seeping in, closely examine decimals **200-299 Religion:** Christian sects subsume over **89** lines of the total **100** slots available, of which **11** are *"no longer used"* leaving only **8** available in which to name *"other religions."* And, thankfully, the headings *evil (216) and prayer (217)* are among those slots *"no longer used."*

Considering the pollution already released since the DDS has been in use, it is difficult to imagine what a desired replacement might be. From a metaspheric perspective, it would need to be divergent (conative) and convergent (cognitive) at the same time.

Consider then Peter Mark Roget's Categorical Imperative

Categorization requires no action or decision. It's like walking into a room unbiased toward the category of ideas called "furniture," prior to pointing out your favorite "chair." It's about a *convergence* of reality prior to separating it out, or *divergence*.

Roget's intuitive imperative was the <u>convergence</u> of ideas

Yes, Roget's *categoration* is a *separating out,* but with the *"undividable one,"* the ultimate sign of *convergence,* likewise intuitively in mind, even after mind has made the first "intellection" called "self" *(review page 73).*

Below are but two examples of the required genius and labor it took for Roget to see all ideas in relation, one to another. These trichotomies are set fouth here as they appear in his intro.

Peter Mark Roget
1779-1869

Roget's main *categories* of ideas, like metasphere, are reduced to two sets of three mutually inclusive ideas. Unlike Dewey's use of 1000 slots, which came decades after Roget's *Synopsis of Categories[1]*, Roget's 1000 slots are utilized in such a way to reveal not only convergence and divergence, but also an *inclusive* vs. *exclusive* outlook on the reality, called world.

INCLUSIVE and naturally unbiased	EXCLUSIVE intentionally biased
ROGET'S TSC[1]	DEWEY or DDC[2]

"The middle column term has a neutral [null] sense in reference to the former.

Identity	Difference	Contrariety
Beginning	Middle	End
Past	Present	Future

The middle column term is simply the negative to each of two opposite terms.

Convexity	Flatness	Concavity
Desire	Indifference	Aversion

The middle term is the standard with which extremes are compared, e.g:

Insufficiency	Sufficiency	Redundance

These forms of correlative expressions would suggest the use of triple, instead of double columns, for tabulating this **threefold** order of words; but the practical inconvenience attending such an arrangement would probably overbalance its advantages."[4]

Roget settled on a two column format using consecutive numbers to indicate correlates.

716. Attack	717. Defence
718. Retaliation	719. Resistance
720. Contention	721. Peace
722. Warfare	723. Pacification

I. ABSTRACT RELATIONS
1-8 Existence
9-24 Relation
25-57 Quantity
58-83 Order 58-83
84-105 Number
106-139 Time
140-152 Change
153-179 Causation

II. SPACE
180-191 General.
192-239 Dimensions
240-263 Form.
264-315 Motion

III. MATTER
316-320 Generally
321-356 Inorganic
357-449 Organic

IV. INTELLECTION
450-515 Formation
516-599 Communication

V. VOLITION
600-736 Individual
737-819 Intersocial

VI. AFFECTION
820-826 Generally
827-887 Personal
888-921 Sympathetic
922-975 Moral
976-1000 Religious

[VII. METARELATION[3]
Relations of relation
Proposed by the author.

GENERAL WORKS
000-099 (types of publication)

100 PHILOSOPHY
100-109 Philosophy
110-119 Metaphysics
120-129 Metaphysical Theory
130-139 Branches of psychology
140-149 Philosophical topics
160-169 Logic
170-179 Ethics
180-189 Ancient & medieval
190-199 Modern philosophy

200 RELIGION
200-289 Christian
290-299 Other religions

300 SOCIAL SCIENCE
300-399 (Types of)

400 LANGUAGE
400-409 Language Theory
410-419 Comparative
420-489 European
490-499 Other languages

500 PURE SCIENCE
500-599 Various

600 TECHNOLOGY
600-699 (types & history)

700 THE ARTS
700-799 (types & history)

800 LITERATURE
800-899 (types & history)

900 HISTORY
900-999 (of civilizations)

---

[1]*Roget's Thesaurus,* 1852 ed p.xxv. [2]*Dewey Decimal Classification,* 8th Ed, p.24. [3]*PartTwo* p.73.
[4]*Roget's Thesaurus,* 1852 ed. p.xiv. [5] Ibid pg xxxv.

Tribute to Franklin Jones' book *The Knee of Listening* (1973)

Mine is one of many tributes to this autobiography of a 34 year old man born in Queens, NY, in 1939. *"What he says, and says very well, is something that I have been trying to say for thirty-five years, but which most people seem reluctant to understand."* - Alan Watts

Aside Watts' Foreword to the book, mine is a simpler tribute:

Unlike many in the 60's, when one had to travel to India to have a guru find them and give them a new name or new life, I had little idea of what a *"guru"* was, much less any desire to meet one. But then Kundalini-Shakti found me, and I took that *presence* to be my guru/teacher. Twenty years later I was surprised that there was a real flesh and blood teacher/guru here in the West.

I was living in Seattle at the time and often enjoyed a Saturday morning browsing the shops in the Washington University district. On one occasion I happened to see a poster announcing a film series coming to a bookstore in the area. A film in the series about Alan Watts (my favorite author of spiritual teachings) caught my eye. That evening I located the bookstore and purchased the movie ticket.

While waiting for the movie to start in the back room, I began to browse the store. Suddenly I felt a familiar shot of Kundalini at the base of my spine, which I had not felt for over a decade. *What just happened?* I turned to the clerk and, as if he knew what happened, I asked "What's this all about." He told me the bookstore specialized in books by a Western-born spiritual adept.

Franklin Jones
1939-2008

He went on to recommend this adept's autobiography, *The Knee of Listening,* by Franklin Jones. No fancy name at the time, simply a man named Jones. I read the book over the next few days and returned to the bookstore, convinced I needed to hear more. The visitation of kundalini-Shakti was certainly a signal, and as Alan Watts said:

"It's obvious, from all sorts of subtle details, that he [Jones] knows what IT's all about ...a rare being."[1]

The long and the short story is that for the next many years I sat with a few hundred others at the knee of this being, as he changed his own name as many times as it took to match the level of his teaching to just beyond his students' level of understanding, but not outside their possible embodiment. Over the three decades of his *Gurudeva* work, perhaps his most recognizable, yet enigmatic, name was simply "Da."

My tribute is less a proselytizing than a celebration of his spiritual genius and divine realization felt and transmitted through his written word in 75 books and listening word in hundreds of video and audio recordings.

What attracted me first was that he called his work *"A Seventh Stage Teaching,"* based on the recognition that there are *"Seven Stages of Life."* Given my obvious interest in septenaries, I was intrigued at the start.

---

[1] See Biblio: 1973, *The Knee Of Listening.*

Tribute to Adi Da Samraj's *"The illusion Of Difference"*

Imagine the *first and seven forms of distinction* [2] not only explained as *something from nothing*, but as the *"illusion of difference"* itself—to see in the esoteric writing below, the exact *"Difference"* mind makes as *"An Un-necessary Fault... (and first ego act)."*

" *'One' Is Not 'Different.'*

'One' Makes No 'Difference.'

'One' Acknowledges No 'Difference.'

'One' Inherently Transcends All 'Difference.'

'One' Effectively Dissolves All 'Difference.'

The mind Makes All The 'Difference.'

The body Is The 'Difference.' " [3]

"The illusion Of Difference"

"The illusion Of 'Difference' (or Of Relatedness, Separateness, and Otherness) Is (Directly and Only) An Apparition, An Un-necessary Fault, and An Utterly Unjustified Presumption (and First ego-Act) Of 'More-Than-One.' Therefore, The (Inherent and Only) One Must Be Realized—Even (At Last) To The Most Perfect Degree of Divine Translation.

"Therefore, The One (Itself) Is Not (Separately) the mind (or attention), or the body, or their (Apparent) relations, results, effects, or causes.

True (Divine—and Inherently, and Most Perfectly, egoless) Freedom is The Condition That (Inherently, Most Perfectly) transcends All 'Difference.'" [3]

Typography Note: *"The [capitalized] words express the Ecstatic "Vision" of Heart-Significance. And the [uncapitalized] words achieve, by their infrequency, a special significance as indicators of the common flow of mind and signal your heart that it is time to Awaken, As you Are."* [4]

Adi Da Samraj
1939-2008

"Notice that at times you speak without thinking at all. There are times—perhaps most of the time—when speech is identical to thought. When you speak without thinking a word before speaking each word, thought does not initiate speech. Then speech is identical to thought. Then thought is speech. Then thought is not inwardness, but action itself." - Prologue, Conscious Exercise and the Transcendental Sun, 1977

---

[2] pp.62-68.   [3] *The Dawn Horse Testament*, 2004, p.1218.   [3] Ibid p.1216.   [4] Typography note, Ibid p.83.

Tribute to the "Anamorphic Eye" in Art and Nature

The Metaspheric Perspective in mind has its analogue in the Anamorphic Perspective in space. Only by finding the "I" in mind and the "eye" in space is either perspective made true and, according to the universal laws of perspective, made the truth of consciousness.

Painting by Felice Varini, *Rectangle, ellipse et disques,* 2010, Galerie Xippas Paris France, www.varini.org

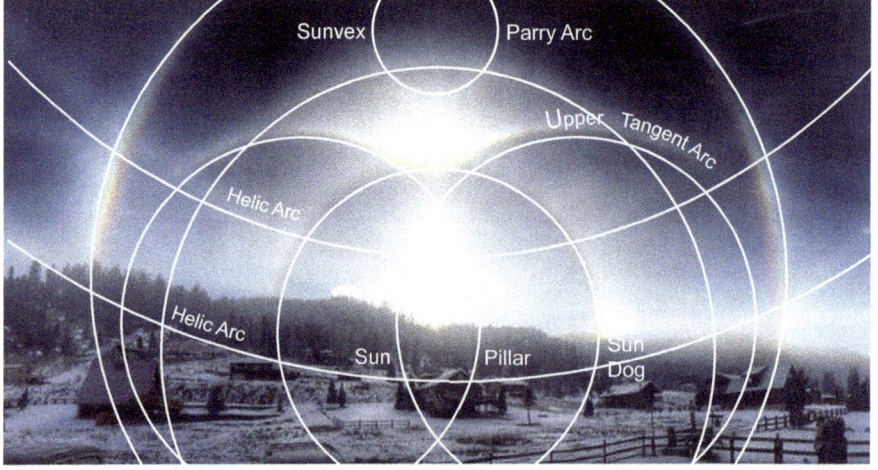

Photo by Joshua Thomas, 2015, (quasi-mind) phenomena at Red River, NM. Orb captions by Les Crowley

Tribute to Charles S. Peirce and "Quasi Mind"

Peirce mentions something he calls *"quasi mind,"* referring to non-human signaling in nature, i.e. *"a sunflower following the signalling of the sun, and the growth of crystals."* Certainly he would include the reflexive *signalling* in light, called color:

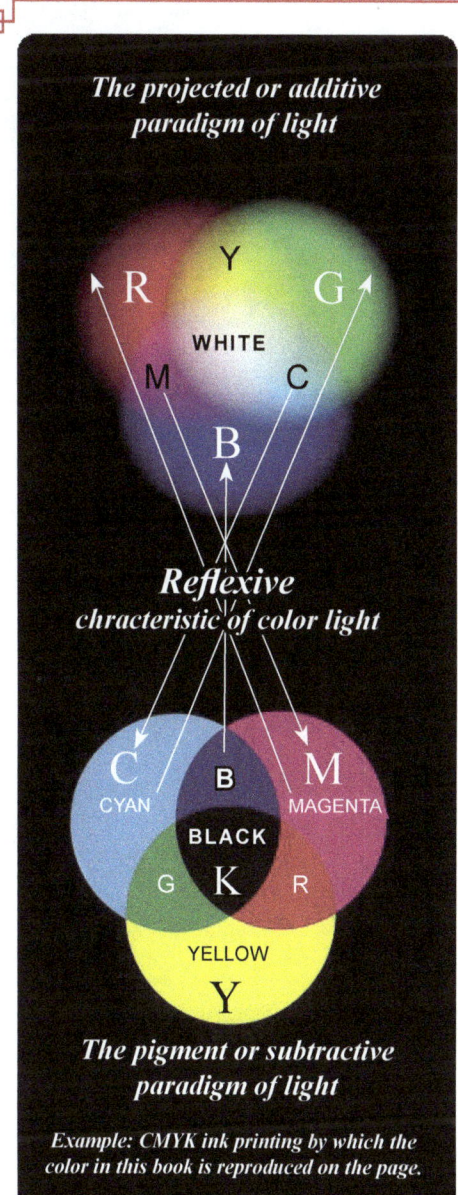

The projected or additive paradigm of light

Reflexive chracteristic of color light

The pigment or subtractive paradigm of light

Example: CMYK ink printing by which the color in this book is reproduced on the page.

Almost hidden in Peirce's cannon of 100,000 pages is this extraordinary statement:

" Thought is not necessarily connected with a brain. It appears in the work of bees, of crystals, and throughout the purely physical world; and one can no more deny that it is really there, than that the colors, the shape, etc., of objects are really there... as there cannot be a general [thing] without instances embodying it, so there cannot be thought without signs."

Certainly analogous to our model of *metasphere* [mind] and *metaspheric perspective* is the reflexive relation between the conventional trichotomies of RGB (red, green, and blue primaries of projected light) and CMY, cyan, magenta, and yellow (secondary or pigment colors). Such an overlapping arrangement, or reflexive characteristic of color (light) also proves that the median of all visible color of light is white and the median of all pigment (reflected) color is black. But most overlooked is a septenary symmetry formed by the central presence of the observer, without which there would be no colors, only light.

Reference

Selected Bibliography

115-119

Index of Illustrations

121

Previous Publications

Recent Presentation Venues

Author Contact Information

123

Selected Bibliography

Entries sorted in order of publication date relative to each of the sections of the book.

PSYCHEDELIC SESSION

Evans-Wentz, W.Y. (1958)
Tibetan Yoga and Secret Doctrines.
Oxford University Press. New York

Aldous Huxley (1960)
Aldous Huxley Collected Essays.
Bantam Books N.Y.

Marghanita Laski (1961)
Ecstasy, in Secular and Religious Experience.
Jeremy P. Tarcher, Inc, Los Angeles,
St. Martin's Press, New York

Timothy Leary. Richard Alpert,
Ralph Metzner (1964)
The Psychedelic Experience:
A Manual Based on the Tibetan
Book of The Dead.
University Books, New York.

Edited by Charles T. Tart (1969)
Altered States of Consciousness.
HaerperCollins Publishers, New York

Ralph Metzner (1971)
Maps of Consciousness: I Ching, Tantra,
Tarot, Alchemy, Astrology.
MacMillan

Chogyam Trungpa (1973)
Cutting Through Spiritual Materialism.
Shambhala Publications, Inc

Stanislav Grof & Joan Halifax Grof (1975)
Realms of The Human Unconscious:
Observations from LSD Research.
The Viking Press, New York

Leary, Timothy (1977)
Exo-Psychology.
Starseed/Peace Press,
Culver City, California

James Guy (1980).
Metasphere: The Altered State of Word.
J. G Lampkin Publishing, Cincinnati, OH

David Jay Brown (2015)
Frontiers of Consciousness: conversations
with Albert Hoffmann, Stanislav Grof, Rick
Strassman, Jeremy Narby, Simon Postfield.
Park Street Press

David Jay Brown (1993)
Mavericks of the Mind, Conversations with
Terence McKenna, Alan Ginsberg, Timothy
Leary, John Lilly, Carolyn Mary Kleefeld,
Laura Huxly, Robert Anton Wilson.
Crossing Press

Alex Grey (2001)
Transfigurations, with contributions by
Albert Hofmann, Stephen Larsen,
Donald, Kuspi, and Ken Wilber.
Shambahala Boston & London

James Oroc (2009)
Tryptamine Palace, 5-MeO-DMT and the
Sonoran Desert Toad.
Park Street Press

James Fadiman, Ph.D. (2011)
The Psychedelic Explorer's Guide,
Safe, Therapeutic, and Sacred Journeys.
Park Street Press

David Jay Brown (2013)
The New Science of Psychedelics,
At the Nexus of Culture, Consciousness,
and Spirituality.
Park Street Press

Mike Crowley (2016)
Secret Drugs of Buddhism: Psychedelic
sacraments and origins of the Vajrayāna.
Amrita Press, Hayfork, California

William A Richards (2016)
Sacred Knowledge, Psychedelics and
Religious Experiences.
Columbia University Press, New York

Allowah Lani, (2016)
Who Am I, Yoga, Psychedelics, and the Quest
for Enlightenment.
CreateSpace/Amazon.com

PSYCHEDELIC CULTURE

Ram Dass (1971).
Remember, Be Here Now.
Lama Foundation. San Cristobal, NM

Pir Vilayat Inayat-Khan (1974)
Toward The One: The Perfection of Love, Harmony, & Beauty, The Only Being
Harper & Row

Art Kleps (1975, revised 2005)
Millbrook, a Narrative of the Early Years of American Psychedelianism.
The Original Kleptonian Neo-American Church

Introduction by R. Buckminster Fuller (1979)
Spiritual Community Guide #4 , The New Consciousness Source Book. Spiritual Community Publications, San Rafael, CA

Don Snyder, (1979)
Aquarian Odyssey: A photographic trip into the sixties,
Liveright, New York

Robert Forte (1997) (2012)
Entheogens and the Future of Religion,
With contributions by Albert Hoffmann, R.Gordon Easson, Jack Kornfield, Terence McKenna, Rick Strassman, and others.
Park Street Press

Georg Feuerstein, Ph.D. (1990,2006)
Holy Madness, Spirituality, Crazy-Wise Teachers, and Enlightenment.
Hohm Press

Alex Grey (1998)
The Mission of Art,
Forword by Ken Wilber,
Shambhala, Boston & London

Ram Dass and Ralph Metzner (2010)
Birth of a Psychedelic Culture:
Conversations about Leary, the Harvard Experiments, Millbrook and the Sixties.
Synergetic Press, Santa Fe, NM

James Fadiman, PhD (2011)
The Psychedelic Explorer's Guide, Safe, Therapeutic, and Sacred Journeys.
Park Street Press

Martin W. Ball, Ph.D. (2017)
Entheogenic Liberation, Unraveling the Enigma of Nonduality with 5-MeO-DMT Energetic Therapy.
Kyandara Publishing

J. Pallamary (2017)
The Center of The Universe Is Right Between Your Eyes, But Home Is Where The Heart Is.
Mystic Ink Publishing

Dick Khan, (2017)
DMT & My Occult Mind, Investigation of occult realities using the spirit molecule.
CreatSpace Independent Publishing

KUNDALINI EXPERIENCE

Carl. G. Jung (1932)
The Psychology of Kundalini Yoga
Notes of the seminar given in 1932 by C. G. Jung, Edited (1996) by Sonu Shamdasani.
Princeton University Press

Woodroffe, Sir John (1959)
Sakti and Sakta.
Ganesh & Company, Madras

Sir John Woodroffe (Arthur Avalon) (1963)
Sādhana for Self-Realization (Mantras, Yantras, and Tantras).
Ganesh & Co., Madras

Carma C. C. Chang (1963)
Teachings of Tibetan Yoga.
University Books

Sir John Woodroffe (Arthur Avalon) (1964)
The Serpent Power.
Ganesh & Company, Madras, India:

Woodroffe, Sir John (1964)
Mahamaya: The world as power, power as consciousness.
Ganish & Co., Madras

Reference

Woodroffe, Sir John (1966)
The World as Power: Reality, Life, Mind, Matter, Causality and Continuity, Ganish & Co., Madras

Gopi Krishna (1971)
Kundalini. The Evolutionary Energy in Man with psychological commentary by James Hillman. Shambhala Publications, Inc.

Manly P. Hall (1972)
Man, The Grand Symbol of the Mysteries, Essays in Occult Anatomy. Philosophical Research Society, Inc,

Philip Rawson (1973)
Tantra, The Indian Cult of Ecstasy. Thames And Hudson, New York

Philip Rawson (1973)
The Art of Tantra.
Thames and Hudson Ltd, London

Charles Ponce (1973)
Kabbalah: An introduction and illumination for the world today.
Straight Arrow Books.

Swami Janakananda Saraswati (1975)
Yoga, Tantra and Meditation
in Your Daily Life.
Ballantine Books NY

Hans-Ulrich Rieker (1974, 1978)
The Yoga of Light: The classic esoteric handbook of Kundalini Yoga.
The Dawn Horse Press

Lee Sannella, M.D., (1976)
Kundalini-Psychosis or Transcendence?
H.S. Dakin Company, San Francisco, CA

Swami Muktananda (1979)
Kundalini: The Secret of Life.
SYDA Foundation

Irena Tweedie (1979)
Chasm of Fire, A woman's experience of liberation through the teachings of a Sufi Master. Element Books

Ajit Mookerje (1982)
Kundalini The Arousal of the Inner Energy.
Destiny Books

Harish Johari (1987)
Chakras: Energy Centers of Transformation.
Destiny Books/Inner Traditions

Jeremy Narby (1998)
The Cosmic Serpent: DNA and the origins of knowledge,
Jeremy P. Tarcher/Putnam

Manly P. Hall, (1988, 1998)
The Secret Teachings of All ages, An Encyclopedia of Masonic, Hermetic, Qabbalistic and Rosicrucian Philosophy.
The Philosophical Research Society, Inc CA

Georg Feuerstein, Ph.D., (1998,2001)
Forword by Ken Wilber
The Yoga Tradition, Its History, Literature, Philosophy and Practice.
Hohm Press

Gabriel Morris (2002)
Kundalini and the Art of Being.
Barrytown, Station Hill

Genevieve Lewis Paulson (2004)
Kundalini and the Chakras, Evolution in this Lifetime, A Practical Guide.
Llewwllyn Publishing, St. Paul, Minnesota

Swami Khecaranatha (2010)
Depth Over Time: Kundalini Maha Yoga: A Path of Transformation and Liberation.
AuthorHouse

PartTwo / Grey Paper

Peter Mark Roget (1852)
Roget's Thesaurus (Introduction to)
Reproduction of First Edition of his Work.
Bloomsbury Books, London

James S. Perkins, (1964)
A Geometry of Space Consciousness.
The Theosophical Publishing House.

Alan W. Watts (1965)
The Joyous Cosmology. Vintage Press

G. Spencer-Brown (1972)
Laws of Form. Crown Publishers,Inc New York

R. Buckminster Fuller (1975)
Synergetics: Exploration in the Geometry of Thinking. McMillan Publishing

Arthur M. Young (1976).
The Reflexive Universe: Evolution of Consciousness. A Merloyd Lawrence Book Delacorte Press

Arthur M. Young (1976)
Geometry of Meaning.
Delacorte Press, New York

Charles Sanders Peirce (1991)
Peirce on Signs: Writings on Semiotics. UNC Press Books.

Buckminster Fuller (1992)
Cosmography, A Posthumous Scenario for the Future of Humanity. by Adjvant Kiyoshi Kuromiya, Macmillan.

John C. Huntington and Dina Bangdel (2003)
The Circle of Bliss: Buddhist Meditational Art. The Ohio State University, Serindia Publications Chicago

TRIBUTE

Peter Mark Roget, M.D. (1852)
Thesaurus of English Words and Phrases. Published in London

Hermann Hesse (1922)
Siddhartha (Transl. Hilda Rosner). New York: New Directions, 1951 New Directions Paperbooks, 1957 Siddhartha. Eine indische Dichtung. Berlin: S. Fischer, 1922

Hermann Hesse (1929)
Steppenwolf (Transl. Basil Creighton.) New York: Holt (1929) Ungar (1957) Random House (1963), Der Steppenwolf. Berlin: S. Fischer, 1927

Hermann Hesse (1932)
Journey to the East. , (Transl. Hilda Rosner.) New York: Noonday Press Paperback, 1957. Translation occasionally amended.)
[Die Morgenlandfahrt. Eine Erz hlung. Berlin: S. Fischer, 1932.]

Hermann Hesse (1945)
Magister Ludi (The Glass Bead Game).
(Translated from the German Das Glassperlanspiel. by Richard and Clara Winston) Bantam Books (1970)

Transcribed from talk by Denis Berry,
International Federation for Internal Freedom (IFIF) Statement of Purpose, 1962, Timothy Leary Archives.org

Editor Ralph Metzner (1963)
The Psychedelic Review, Vol. 1, No. 1,
(Article) Statement of Purpose IFIF

Editor Ralph Metzner (1963)
The Psychedelic Review, Vol. 1, No. 2,
(Article) Hermann Hesse, Poet of the Internal Journey

Franklin Jones (1973)
The Knee of Listening, An Autobiography, Dawn Horse Press, Clearlake CA

Timothy Leary (1983)
Flashbacks, An Autobiography, J.P. Tarcher, Inc

Rene Daumal (1986)
Mount Analogue.
Boston: Shambhala Nakamura, Hajime

Buckminster Fuller (1992)
Cosmography, A Posthumous Scenario for the Future of Humanity by Adjvant Kiyoshi Kuromiya. Macmillan.

C. Michael Smith (1994)
Jung and Shamanism in Dialogue:
Retrieving the Soul / Retrieving the Sacred. Paulist Press, Mahwah, NJ

Timothy Leary Ph.D. (1996)
The Politics of Ecstasy, (Chapter) Hermann Hesse: Politics of the Interior Journey. Ronin Publishing

Adi Da Samraj (2004)
The Dawn Horse Testament of The Ruchira Avatar. (Supercedes all previous editions since 1985. Dawn Horse Press, Middletown, CA, Standard Edition, enlarged and updated

GENERAL

Ancient text (Mid 2nd to 1st Millenium BCE)
The Ribhu Gita, The First Complete Edition English Translation, 2009.
Sri Ramanasramam Tiruvannamalai, India

Rudolf Hermann Lotze (1884).
Logic: in three books, of thought, of investigation, and of knowledge
(translation by Bernard Bosanquet
Oxford: Clarendon.

Sepharial (1911)
The Kabala of Numbers.
London: Rider

Nigel Calder (1977)
Key To The Universe.
New York: Viking Penguin Inc.

György Doczi (1981)
The Power of Limits, Proportional Harmonies in Nature, Art & Architecture.
Shambhala

José Argüelles, Ph.D. (1988)
Earth Ascending, An illustrated treatise on the law governing whole systems,
Forword by Charles T. Tart
Bear & Co, Santa Fe, New Mexico

Lex Hixon (1993)
Mother of the Buddhas, Meditation on the prajnaparamita Sutra, Forword by Robert Thurman, Ph.D.
Quest Books

Lex Hixon (1994)
Mother of the Universe, Visions of the Goddess and Tantric Hymns of Enlightenment.
Quest Books

Michael S. Schneider (1994)
A Beginner's Guide to Constructing The Universe: The Mathematical Archetypes of Nature, Art, and Science.
Harper Collins Publishers

Burton Daniels (2002)
The Integration of Psyche and Spirit, Essays Reconciling Psychology and Spirituality. Writers Showcase, New York

Ervin Lazlo (2004, Second Edition 2007)
Science and the Akashic Field The Integral Theory of Everything, Inner Traditions

Colin Wilson (2009)
Super Consciousness,
The Quest for the Peak Experience.
Watkins Publishing

Robin Robertson, Ph.D, (2009)
Indra's Net, Alchemy and Chaos Theory as Models for Transformation. Quest Books

Peter Bauman and Michael W. Taft (2011)
Ego, The fall of the twin towers and the rise of an enlightened humanity.,
NE Press, San Francisco

Mark Friedman (2012)
The Origin of Consciousness, The Natural Selection of Choice-Making Systems.
Parse Publishing,

Antonin Tuynman Ph.D. (2016)
Technovedanta 2.0, Transcendental Metaphysics.
Rijwijk, Netherlands

DESK REFERENCE

Peter Mark Roget 1852
Thesaurus of English Words and Phrases.
(facsimily of original edition)
Blumsbury Books, London

Ernest Weekley (1967)
An Etymological Dictionary of Modern English
(Two Volumes)
Dover, New York

Michael H. Kohn, (1991)
The Shambhala Dictionary of Buddhism and Zen.
Shambhala, Boston

Editors (1994)
The Encyclopedia of Eastern Philosophy and Religion:
Buddhism, Hinduism, Taoism, Zen.
Shambhala, Boston,

Reference 121

Index of Illustrations and Panels
*Entries by page numbers in order of appearance
and relative to each section of the book:*

PartOne

3 What is "set" and "setting" (Richard Alpert)
4 Castalia at Millbrook (Photo of Mansion)
5 First News of the first research (books)
9 Entheogenic Vision
11 What is Paranoia?
13 Castalia at Millbrook (Photo of Tim)
15 Letter from Tim Leary
17 What is merging?
19 What is a flashback?
21 Parable about Presence
22 Ladder to Godhood
23 Ladder to Egohood
24 Cutting Through (photo of Trungpa)
25 The cosmic joke
26 The Abhidhamma
29 Chakra tantra painting
31 Kundalini yogic pose
33 Tour of energy nadis and channels
35 Primal/future recapitulation
36 Yab-yum
3 Feeling observation of kundalini
39 The whole picture
41 Be here Now (Photo of Ram Dass)
42 Toward the One (photo of Pir Vilayat)

PartTwo

44 Photos of phenomenologist outliers
48 Polarity of letter "N"
49 1st, 2nd, 3rd Person Deixis
51 Repurposed wood cut (verbal curtain)
53 Scriptura Continua (example)
55 True outlier (photo of Peirce)
57 Venn proof of metasphere
59 Modes of mind
60 Metaspherical vs linear model
61 Booting up (gear)
65 Laws of Form (photo of Spencer-Brown)

63 Excerpt from Randy Dible's paper
73 "Eye" to "I" Analogue
66-67 metapheric distinctions
68 Legend to 66-67
69 The Reflexive Universe (Young)
70 Young's "Arc of process"
71 Young's "The Grid"
72 A glossary of terms
73 Roget's categories of ideas
74-75 Montage of symmetry in myth
75 Standard model of matter
76 Clockwork escapement mechanism
76 Consciousness, map, territory
78-79 alternate of page 66-67

PartThree

80 Glass beads on thread
83 The Gameboard
84-93 Screen shots of game app

Tribute

94 Hermann Hesse
103 C. Michael Smith
104 Böhme's "Philofophic Globe" 1620AD
105 Fuller's "Tetrahedral" Universe"
105 Réne Dumal's "Surreal Universe"
106 Dewy versus Roget systems
107 Roget's categorical imperative
108 Franklin Jones, Knee of Listening
109 Adi Da Samraj, "The illusion of Difference"
110 Varini's "Anamorphic Eye"
111 Charles S. Peirce, "Quasi Mind"

Cover
Man gazing at ice shelf (stock photo)
photoshopped by author. Cover layout
by College Publishing designer.

Previous Publications

WHAT ALWAYS COMES TO MIND
The Visualist's Guide to a Metaspheric Perspective on Reality
(2016) ISBN 978-0-692-76878-5, 228 pages. Contains an elaboration of defuse preliminary research, which has been consolidated, simplified, and shortened in this, the subsequent (2024) 138 page title, *Toward Repurposing Mind.*

METASPHERE The Altered State of Heart
A visual-music ani-meditation on kundalini, self guided, no vocal.
(2007) DVD, 8 4284108894 2, Available from Kunaki, LLC.
Theatrical screening available, contact author.

METASPHERE The Altered State of Word
An anthology of mystic thought and symbolic geometries.
(1980) ISBN 0 9604918 72, LOC Catalog Number 80-83463 7 2 (136 pages).
Out of print, a few remnant copies available from author.

Recent Presentation Venues

2023, THINKING THE FLOAT TANK
2023 Conference August 24-26. West Den Hagg, in the Museum For Contemporary Art, the Netherlands. Commemorating: The AUM Fiftieth Anniversary Conference; on Cybernetics, Float Tanks and Phenomenology. My 2023 remote presentation was titled *Metaspheric Perspective - Navigating mind from the first-person point-of-view.*

2018, THE SCIENCE OF CONSCIOUSNESS
"Is the Self/Other Reflex of Conative-Mind Evolutionarily Obsolete?"
2018 Conference, April 2-7 Loews Ventana Canyon Resort Tucson AZ, USA.
See abstract in conference proceedings book, under conference heading:
Experiential Approaches, 5.01, Phenomenology, entry 258. page 165.
Poster Session indexed (P2) p.29.

2017, PSYCHEDELIC SCIENCE
"Beyond Entheogenic Mind: Repurposing Our Evolutionarily Obsolete Self//Other Consciousness"
Conference, April 19-24 Oakland Merriott City Center, CA USA
(Oral paper) Psymposia Stage, Main hall.

Author Contact Information
jamesguy@metasphere.org

FirstThought

AfterThought

www.ingramcontent.com/pod-product-compliance
Lightning Source LLC
Chambersburg PA
CBHW050833160426
43192CB00010B/2004